Coding with XML for Efficiencies in Cataloguing and Metadata

Every purchase of a Facet book helps to fund CILIP's advocacy,
awareness and accreditation programmes
for information professionals.

Coding with XML for Efficiencies in Cataloguing and Metadata

Practical applications of XSD, XSLT, and XQuery

Timothy W. Cole

Myung-Ja (MJ) K. Han

Christine Schwartz

© American Library Association, 2018

Published by Facet Publishing,
7 Ridgmount Street, London WC1E 7AE
www.facetpublishing.co.uk

Facet Publishing is wholly owned by CILIP: the Chartered Institute of Library and Information Professionals.

Except as otherwise permitted under the Copyright, Designs and Patents Act 1988 this publication may only be reproduced, stored or transmitted in any form or by any means, with the prior permission of the publisher, or, in the case of reprographic reproduction, in accordance with the terms of a licence issued by The Copyright Licensing Agency. Enquiries concerning reproduction outside those terms should be sent to Facet Publishing, 7 Ridgmount Street, London WC1E 7AE.

First published in the USA by
the American Library Association, 2018.
This UK edition 2018.

British Library Cataloguing in Publication Data
A catalogue record for this book is available from the British Library.

ISBN 978-1-78330-369-4

Printed and bound in the United Kingdom by Lightning Source.

CONTENTS

PREFACE

This volume is a direct outgrowth of an all-day pre-conference workshop (www.ala.org/alcts/events/ac/2015/coding) held on June 25, 2015 at the Moscone Convention Center, San Francisco, in conjunction with that year's Annual Conference of the American Library Association (ALA). The workshop was entitled "Coding for Efficiencies in Cataloging and Metadata: Practical Applications of XML, XSLT, XQuery, and PyMarc for Library Data." The workshop was sponsored by the ALA's Association for Library Collections & Technical Services (ALCTS) and cosponsored by the ALA's Library and Information Technology Association (LITA) Program Planning Committee and the Online Audiovisual Catalogers, Inc. The presenters were Timothy W. Cole, Myung-Ja K. Han, Christine Schwartz, and Heidi Frank.

At the end of the day, the consensus of the presenters was that there hadn't been time enough to share with the audience, primarily catalogers and metadata librarians, everything they collectively wanted the audience to know about Extensible Markup Language (XML) and how to use it in their work. This was not really unexpected. XML and its ancillary technologies, XML Schema (XSD), the Extensible Stylesheet Language for Transformations (XSLT), and the XML Query Language (XQuery), encompass a great deal of material, and there's only so much that can be covered in a single-day workshop. The sense that more was needed, combined with the generally positive response to the workshop, led directly to the decision to write this book. The coauthors of this book include three of the four presenters from the 2015 pre-conference workshop (the workshop coverage of PyMarc is not included in this volume).

The goal of this volume is to introduce and illustrate concretely a few of the ways that XML technologies can be used in library cataloging and metadata management settings to enhance workflow effectiveness and efficiency. While still not comprehensive, the material covered in this volume provides a solid foundation for librarians and library staff who are beginning to or are ready to integrate XML and its related technologies into their day-to-day work. While some prior exposure to XML is helpful, we start with a review of the basics of what XML is and how it is used in library cataloging and metadata workflows, and then move on to talk about workflows for validating XML metadata records, transforming XML metadata into HTML and to meet other kinds of workflow objectives, and querying collections of XML metadata records using XQuery. The final chapter provides information about additional resources for readers who are interested in learning more about advanced concepts, use cases, and techniques. Two of the authors also maintain public GitHub repositories which include XSLT (https://github.com/tcole3/XSLT/) or XQuery (https://github.com/caschwartz) examples.

This is a work written by practitioners, intended for practitioners and especially for librarians new to the field who need to come up to speed quickly on XML and how it is used by libraries today. While by no means the only technology arrow in a modern-day cataloger's or metadata librarian's knowledge and skills quiver, a firm understanding of XML remains relevant and helpful for those working in modern bibliographic control or with information discovery services. We hope you find this volume a useful resource, worthy of a place on your reference bookshelf.

ACKNOWLEDGMENTS

We must begin by acknowledging the members of the ALCTS Technical Services Workflows Efficiency Interest Group and in particular Annie Glerum and Michael Winecoff, who were cochairs of the Interest Group in the spring of 2014 when the group came up with the idea of doing a practical pre-conference workshop on XML for catalogers at the ALA's 2015 Annual Conference. Annie and Michael assembled the speakers for the workshop, and with the assistance of Annie's colleague Dominique Bortmas and ALCTS staff (notably Julie Reese and Emily Whitmore), Annie and Michael expertly coordinated workshop logistics from the proposal all the way through to the actual event, helping to ensure the success of the workshop. Without their help this book would not have been written.

We would also like to acknowledge our collaborators over the years with whom we learned about, explored, and eventually became experts in XML and its ancillary technologies. At the University of Illinois at Urbana-Champaign (home institution for Myung-Jan K. Han and Timothy W. Cole), this includes collaborators on the Emblematica Online project, the source for the workflow examples discussed in chapter 7, and especially Mara Wade and Janina Sarol, without whose collaboration we wouldn't have had such a rich illustration of the power of XML. We learn best through collaboration and doing.

INTRODUCTION

The Extensible Markup Language (XML) was introduced by the World Wide Web Consortium (W3C) in 1998.[1] XML, a web-friendly subset of the preexisting Standard General Markup Language (SGML), was developed to facilitate the creation, use, and sharing (especially on the Web) of structured information. It is intentionally similar to the HyperText Markup Language (HTML), albeit more general-purpose, and is less focused on the presentation of information to users than is HTML. Libraries and publishers have widely adopted XML as a way to serialize and exchange bibliographic catalog records and other kinds of structured metadata about the books, special collection items, and other resources they produce, hold, or license. Because of its rigor and underlying approach to modeling structured information like metadata, libraries immediately found XML helpful, but on its own the XML standard is insufficient for developing efficient and general utility workflows that update, analyze, or otherwise process metadata to support library services and interoperability between libraries. Additional extensions and standards were needed (and were created) to support the construction and development of useful XML applications and workflows, that is, to create a full-featured XML ecosystem.

This volume is designed to introduce the XML Schema Definition language (XSD), the Extensible Stylesheet Language for Transformations (XSLT), and the XML Query language (XQuery) to catalogers, metadata librarians, developers, library science students, and others within the library and information science domain who are involved in creating, developing, or otherwise working with catalog record and metadata processing workflows. This introduction is meant to be practical and concrete, and our goal is to inform largely through illustrations drawn from our collective experiences in libraries working with catalog records and metadata in XML.

This volume is an outgrowth of an ALA Annual Conference pre-conference workshop held in San Francisco in June 2015 (www.ala.org/alcts/events/ac/2015/coding). Our objectives in writing this book, as they were in giving the workshop, are to describe and illustrate by example the means and methods of using XSLT and/or XQuery to edit metadata at scale, to streamline and scale up metadata and cataloging workflows, and to extract, manipulate, and construct MARC records and other formats and types of library metadata. We anticipate that this book will be most useful to readers who have encountered XML already in their work or studies, or who are at least familiar with another, related markup language such as HTML. Prior experience with XSD, XSLT, XPath, or XQuery is not required. Some familiarity with the Library of Congress MARC 21 format for bibliographic data (https://www.loc.gov/marc/bibliographic/) will help readers get the most from the examples and illustrations, but it is not expected that every reader will be a MARC expert or full-time MARC cataloger. Similarly, some familiarity with scripting or similar low-level programming is helpful, but not essential. This book is organized and designed to help even XML newbies get started using XSD, XSLT, and XQuery.

HOW THIS BOOK IS ORGANIZED

Depending on your level of experience with XML and library metadata, you'll find that the first third of this volume is either an introduction or a refresher. Chapter 2, "A Quick Review of XML Basics," spans the basics of XML terminology and the XML data model, starting from first principles and covering the differences between markup and content, elements and attributes, and well-formed and valid XML. The objective of chapter 2 is to lay a solid, shared foundation for reading the rest of the book. Chapter 3, "Library Metadata in XML," illustrates with examples how common, standard descriptive metadata schemes used in libraries today can be expressed using XML syntax and

XML-compatible semantics. Chapter 4, "XML Validation Using Schemas," introduces the XML Schema Definition language (XSD) and demonstrates how XSD files can be used to help validate the structure and semantics of XML metadata records that purport to conform to a specific metadata format or standard. While an understanding of XSD is not a prerequisite for using XSLT or XQuery, in practice most cataloging or metadata workflows include validation and quality control components, and XSD is a useful tool when building such workflow components. In addition, an examination of the XSD associated with a particular metadata format makes the creation and development of XSLT and XQuery workflow steps easier by exposing the full range of structures and semantics that can be encountered in a collection of metadata records.

Most of the rest of the book, chapters 5 through 11, focuses on the practical uses of XSLT and XQuery. Chapter 5, "An Introduction to XPath and XSLT," provides an overview of the XML Path Language (which is foundational for both XSLT and XQuery) and an introduction to creating XSLT stylesheets for manipulating and transforming XML metadata records. Chapters 6 and 7 illustrate the use of XSLT in concrete library workflows. Chapters 8 and 9 introduce XQuery and basic library use cases involving XQuery. Chapter 10 looks at the use of functions in XQuery scenarios, and chapter 11 describes how XQuery is used for a metadata workflow that helps to create submission files for the HathiTrust Digital Library. Finally, chapter 12 provides links to additional resources for the reader wanting to learn more about the advanced features of these technologies.

While containing elements of both, this book is less a ready-reference than a tutorial on its subject. As discussed in chapter 12, the best ready-reference for XSD, XSLT, and XQuery when developing library cataloging or metadata workflows is the Web. The challenge is knowing enough to enter the correct search to find the XPath expression, XSLT instruction, or XQuery function call that will meet your need. This book is intended to give you that needed initial knowledge and to provide you with practical examples and starting points.

XML TOOLS

Readers are encouraged to delve deeper into and extend the examples and illustrations provided in this book as they read. There is no substitute for hands-on work with XML, XSD, XSLT, and XQuery when trying to learn and appreciate the nuances and functionalities of these technologies. Trial and error is an excellent teacher in this domain. As discussed in chapter 12, there are a number of excellent tutorial and reference resources online that can be used to expand on and elaborate the basic discussions found in this book of the syntax and semantics of these standards. Appendix D, "Configurations for Working with XML, XSD, XSLT and XQuery," which is based on instructions created for the workshop, provides tips for installing useful tools and setting up your environment for working with XML. When it comes to tools for creating, editing, viewing, and manipulating XML metadata, the reader has a number of good options available, both desktop-based and online.

Relatively little infrastructure is required to get started with XML. Files can be created using almost any plain text editor (e.g., Microsoft Notepad, distributed with Windows; TextEdit, distributed with the Apple operating systems; and gedit, a GNOME core application that is ubiquitous on Linux-based computers). Because UTF-8 (the 8-bit version of the Unicode Transformation Format) is the default character encoding for XML, it is even possible to embed non-keyboard characters in your XML using a plain text editor. (But beware of word processors that may use non-Unicode character encodings and special formatting for certain characters, e.g., word processor-specific quote marks, dashes, and the like. These will be displayed differently in an XML-aware application.) Once created and stored on your computer workstation, XML documents can be viewed (and checked for syntax conformance) using most modern web browsers. Figure 1.1 shows a simplified MARC 21 XML record with no associated style information as viewed in a web browser. As mentioned in chapter 5, most web browsers can even process a limited set of XPath expressions and XSLT instructions.

However, for any significant work with XML, XSD, XSLT, and XQuery, XML-specific tools are essential. Chapter 12 includes links to several websites for XML-specific tools, most of which are free, relatively inexpensive, or at least have relatively inexpensive educational/noncommercial purchase or licensing options available. XML editors, parsers, XQuery processors, transformation engines, and similar tool suites—for example, the SyncRO Soft oXygen XML editor, the Altova XMLSpy editor and development environment, and the IVI Technologies Stylus Studio X16 XML enterprise tool suite, to name just three available options—greatly facilitate the creation and development of XML, XSLT, and XQuery documents. These full-featured XML tools provide interfaces that are optimized for creating and editing XML documents, generating and validating XML schemas (XSD files), and developing and testing XSLT stylesheets and XQuery code. Most tools support multiple versions of these standards, including the most recent and up-to-date versions. When editing or creating an XML document that conforms to a particular XSD, these

This XML file does not appear to have any style information associated with it. The document tree is shown below.


```
▼<record>
   <leader>01698cam 22003614a 4500</leader>
   <controlfield tag="001">5439928</controlfield>
   <controlfield tag="005">20080104135038.0</controlfield>
   <controlfield tag="008">070313s2007 ctua b 001 0 eng</controlfield>
  ▼<datafield tag="010" ind1=" " ind2=" ">
     <subfield code="a">2007009006</subfield>
   </datafield>
  ▼<datafield tag="020" ind1=" " ind2=" ">
     <subfield code="a">9781591582809 (alk. paper)</subfield>
   </datafield>
  ▼<datafield tag="020" ind1=" " ind2=" ">
     <subfield code="a">1591582806 (alk. paper)</subfield>
   </datafield>
  ▼<datafield tag="029" ind1="1" ind2=" ">
     <subfield code="a">NLGGC</subfield>
     <subfield code="b">302541152</subfield>
   </datafield>
  ▼<datafield tag="035" ind1=" " ind2=" ">
     <subfield code="a">(OCoLC)ocn105428765</subfield>
   </datafield>
  ▼<datafield tag="050" ind1="0" ind2="0">
     <subfield code="a">Z666.7</subfield>
     <subfield code="b">.C65 2007</subfield>
   </datafield>
  ▼<datafield tag="100" ind1="1" ind2=" ">
     <subfield code="a">Cole, Timothy W.</subfield>
   </datafield>
  ▼<datafield tag="245" ind1="1" ind2="0">
    ▼<subfield code="a">
       Using the Open Archives Initiative Protocol for Metadata Harvesting.
     </subfield>
     <subfield code="c">Timothy W. Cole and Muriel Foulonneau</subfield>
   </datafield>
  ▼<datafield tag="260" ind1=" " ind2=" ">
     <subfield code="a">Westport, Conn. :</subfield>
     <subfield code="b">Libraries Unlimited,</subfield>
     <subfield code="c">c2007.</subfield>
   </datafield>
  ▼<datafield tag="300" ind1=" " ind2=" ">
     <subfield code="a">xv, 208 p. :</subfield>
     <subfield code="b">ill. ;</subfield>
     <subfield code="c">26 cm.</subfield>
   </datafield>
  ▼<datafield tag="440" ind1=" " ind2="0">
     <subfield code="a">Third millennium cataloging</subfield>
   </datafield>
  ▼<datafield tag="650" ind1=" " ind2="0">
     <subfield code="a">Metadata harvesting.</subfield>
   </datafield>
  ▼<datafield tag="610" ind1="2" ind2="0">
     <subfield code="a">Open Archives Initiative.</subfield>
   </datafield>
  ▼<datafield tag="700" ind1="1" ind2=" ">
     <subfield code="a">Foulonneau, Muriel</subfield>
   </datafield>
 </record>
```


Figure 1.1 | **A simplified MARC XML record viewed in a web browser**

tools provide hints and suggestions on screen as you type. Typos and errors in XSLT code are immediately highlighted as you type. Specialized views also are provided for creating and testing XSLT snippets and XQuery expressions.

In addition, for library developers and other programmers, most current scripting and programming languages (e.g., Python, JavaScript, VB.NET, Java) provide libraries with stable application programming interfaces (APIs) for generating and manipulating XML programmatically and for invoking XSLT and XQuery from within your code. This makes it feasible to use, transform, and query XML metadata records at scale and in batch mode.

The essential takeaway from this book is that learning and using XML, XSD, XSLT, and XQuery technologies enables librarians and developers to take advantage of powerful, XML-aware applications, facilitates the interoperability and sharing of XML metadata, and makes it possible to realize the full promise of XML to support more powerful and more efficient library cataloging and metadata workflows.

Note

1. Tim Bray, Jean Paoli, C. M. Sperberg-McQueen, Eve Maler, and François Yergeau, eds., *W3C Recommendation: Extensible Markup Language (XML) 1.0,* 5th edition (Cambridge, MA: Massachusetts Institute of Technology, 2008), www.w3.org/TR/xml/.

A QUICK REVIEW OF XML BASICS

Markup languages reveal the structure of information resources. Knowledge of this structure can help a computer application optimize the way information is processed and displayed. For example, web browsers rely in part on the document structure exposed by the HyperText Markup Language (HTML) to know how to format a web page appropriately for the device you are using. Using XML to reveal the structure of a metadata record or other information resource can achieve multiple goals:

- it can enhance search precision;
- it can facilitate the collation of related information resources;
- it can make it easier to identify, differentiate, select, and extract information for ingestion into a database; and
- it can facilitate interoperability.

Markup can reveal and make explicit to a computer application various semantic relationships within and between resources, thereby facilitating automated inferencing and advanced information processing. So, how do markup languages like XML expose structure?

FIRST PRINCIPLES
Ordered Hierarchy of Content Objects

The underlying assumption of markup languages like HTML and XML is that textual information can be modeled as an Ordered Hierarchy of Content Objects (OHCO; an example of a tree data structure in computer science).[1] For instance, the full text of a book might be defined as containing three types of top-level content objects: FrontMatter, Chapter(s), and BackMatter. A FrontMatter object might in turn contain Title, Author(s), and Publication Information content objects. A Chapter might contain Paragraph(s), Table(s), and Figure(s). A Paragraph might contain Sentence(s). And so on. Given this perspective, the full text of a digitized book can be serialized as an ordered hierarchy of content objects. The World Wide Web Consortium (W3C) XML Recommendation defines rules (syntax) for marking up (i.e., serializing) information in accord with the OHCO data model.[2]

In contrast to HTML, which, though it also follows the OHCO data model, limits itself to a fixed set of content object labels (i.e., fixed semantics) and a fixed hierarchical structure, XML is a meta-markup language in that it includes mechanisms for defining your own content object labels (semantics), hierarchy, and content models. (Content models constrain exactly what each type of content object may contain.) Using XML, the same information can be marked up in multiple ways. This flexibility is both a strength and a limitation of XML. Labels, hierarchy, and content models can be selected and defined in accordance with intended use cases. This is a strength of XML. But illustrative of a limitation, interoperability can suffer if different implementers use different labels and content models, especially if content models assume different content object granularities. Generally, though, in the context of library metadata, XML with its OHCO data model is a natural fit for the highly structured information that is prevalent in catalog records and other forms of resource descriptions. XML supports the recognition, indexing, and reuse of the components found in library metadata and catalog records; for example, book title, author name(s), publication information, and so on. Adhering to XML syntax facilitates random access to metadata elements. Assuming that your metadata markup scheme requires each record to have a clearly labeled unique identifier, XML metadata are easy to manage. Assuming you use recognized authorities and select a scheme with sound semantics and content models, your XML metadata can be used to build indexes supportive of robust search, to create rich metadata displays for human readers, to generate text snippets formatted for inclusion in a journal article bibliography, and so on.

There are limitations, of course. The OHCO data model assumes that an XML document instance hierarchy has a single root content object and does not allow overlap within the hierarchy. For example, in marking up a full-text book, you may want to expose both the paragraph and page structure of the book; however, some paragraphs will cross page boundaries, violating the non-overlapping constraints of the OHCO data model. (There are workarounds and this is generally not a significant impediment for metadata markup.) In most library metadata contexts, the expressiveness and functional limitations of the OHCO approach to markup are negligible. On the whole, XML and its inherent OHCO model work well as a way to serialize library metadata.

Nor is OHCO the entire story. There is more to metadata workflows than simply exposing and labeling the structure of a catalog record. XML syntax on its own is not a sufficient solution. Ancillary standards are required to describe how to display and manipulate XML metadata (e.g., transform XML metadata into HTML). This adds complexity. Fortunately, the required ancillary standards, as well as tools based on these standards, exist (as we illustrate in subsequent chapters). But XML syntax is the foundation on which these ancillary standards are based. So in the rest of this chapter we describe the core syntax of XML and illustrate this syntax with a few examples. Libraries continue to use XML for metadata, even as, with an eye to the future, they also investigate complementary technologies (e.g., JavaScript Object Notation [JSON]).

DIVIDING THE WORLD INTO CONTENT AND MARKUP

In XML, there is content and there is markup. Markup is added to expose the structure of the content. Content in XML documents consists of parsed character data (PCData); for example, text, numbers, and references to special characters and non-textual information (entities). By default, PCData is encoded in UTF-8.[3] (Metadata encoded using the MARC-8 standard is converted to UTF-8 for inclusion in XML.[4]) Markup consists of Elements, Attributes, Comments, and Processing Instructions; these are discussed below. In XML, markup is set apart from content by angle brackets ('<' and '>'), with the exception that certain content may be included within angle brackets as unparsed strings (CDATA) or as the value of an XML Attribute. Figure 2.1 shows a simple example of bibliographic metadata serialized as XML. The content here is all PCData: the title of the book, the names of the authors, the name of the publisher, and the publication date. The string "`2013-04-01`,"

```
<?xml version="1.0" encoding="UTF-8"?>
<CatalogRecord>
    <BookTitle>XML for Catalogers and Metadata Librarians</BookTitle>
    <Author order="2">M. J. Han</Author>
    <Author order="1">Tim Cole</Author>
    <Publisher>Libraries Unlimited</Publisher>
    <PublicationDate w3cdtf="2013-04-01">April 2013</PublicationDate>
</CatalogRecord>
```

Figure 2.1 | **A simple, well-formed XML metadata record**

serialized as an attribute value in this example (more on this syntax later), is provided as an alternate way to express the `<PublicationDate>` element's content, "`April 2013`." Everything else in figure 2.1 is XML markup.

HOW DOES XML COMPARE TO HTML?

As alluded to above, HTML is itself a markup language. So why not just serialize library metadata in HTML? This can be done, of course, but there are drawbacks to such an approach. First, HTML is a display-oriented scheme for making web pages. It is designed to expose structure useful for display. HTML has a fixed set of element and attribute names. It lacks explicit labels and semantics that are useful for describing resources in libraries; for example, there are no HTML labels explicitly intended to contain content like subject headings, call number, place of publication, and so on, and HTML is not easily extensible. The best you can do is rely on conventions (e.g., agree to always put author names, and nothing else, in `<emph>` elements nested within `<h2>` elements). Such an approach is difficult to scale or maintain and quickly becomes unworkable for metadata of any complexity or diversity. XML, on the other hand, is highly extensible. In XML, system designers can define all the element and attribute names they need for their application. HTML has the advantage of default rules for displaying content, but with today's stylesheet languages (e.g., the Cascading Style Sheet [CSS] language), most developers override these default display behaviors anyway, and CSS can be used with XML as easily as with HTML. So the extensibility and flexibility of XML makes more sense when it comes to serializing library metadata, but there are tradeoffs.

XML syntax is stricter than HTML syntax (catalogers sometimes appreciate this since it can reduce ambiguity). This requires more care when authoring XML, but it also facilitates robust validation. In practice, many libraries use XML behind the scenes for certain workflows and then transform their XML metadata into HTML dynamically at the point of presenting metadata to library users. Among the ways in which XML is stricter than HTML are the following:

- In XML markup labels (e.g., Element and Attribute names) are case-sensitive.
- Attribute values must always be enclosed in quotes.
- Attributes must always have a value.
- Elements must always be explicitly closed (i.e., have a close tag as discussed below).
- XML does not include predefined character references or entities (described below) other than for '<,' '>,' '&,' and quotes (both single and double).

XML ELEMENTS

Elements are at the core of XML syntax. Elements delineate content objects. In XML, there are exactly four kinds of content models that can apply to an element:

1. Element content model (the element may only contain other elements)
2. PCData content model (element content is a parsed character string)
3. Mixed content model (may contain other elements with PCData interspersed)
4. Empty content model (may not contain any content; see an example below)

The element and mixed content models expose structural hierarchy through nesting. Figure 2.2 shows an XML fragment illustrating how elements may be nested (i.e., appear within other elements) to convey the hierarchical nature of metadata, in this case publication information. The following XML elements appear in this illustration: `<pubInfo>`, `<publisherName>`, `<placeOfPublication>`, `<yearOfPublication>`, `<city>`, and `<country>`. The elements `<placeOfPublication>` and `<pubInfo>` have element content models, while the other elements have PCData content models. XML element hierarchy is often represented graphically as a simple tree in two dimensions; elements are nodes in this tree view. Nodes with element or mixed content models may create branches in the tree hierarchy, with the terminal node of

```
<pubInfo>
    <publisherName>ABC-CLIO (Libraries Unlimited)</publisherName>
    <placeOfPublication>
        <city>Santa Barbara</city>
        <country>USA</country>
    </placeOfPublication>
    <yearOfPublication>2013</yearOfPublication>
</pubInfo>
```

Figure 2.2 | **An XML fragment illustrating element nesting**

each branch then being called a "leaf node." The element <pubInfo> is at the root of this XML fragment's hierarchy. The elements <publisherName>, <yearOfPublication>, and <placeOfPublication> are all at the second level of the element hierarchy, with the first two of these also being leaf nodes. The elements <city> and <country> are at the third level of the hierarchy and also are terminal leaf nodes. As illustrated here, branches of the tree's hierarchy do not have to be (and rarely are) of equal length.

Notice also that in figure 2.2 each element name appears an even number of times. Here the markup structure containing the first occurrence of an element name, that is, without the leading '/' character, is referred to as a start tag. With the exception of empty elements, every start tag must have a matching close tag. The element name also appears in the close tag where it is preceded by a '/' character. The W3C XML Recommendation defines rules for element names; for example, element names may not contain spaces. As discussed below, an element start tag may contain more than just the element name; for example, Attributes, as illustrated in figure 2.1.

Empty elements are supported in XML. Empty elements contain no content. They may appear in an XML metadata record because the element is required to be present by the markup scheme even when no value is available for a particular metadata record. For example, if the year of publication were unknown in the figure 2.2 illustration, this element might appear as:

```
<yearOfPublication></yearOfPublication>
```

Or an empty element may be a placeholder for content stored separately; for example, as the <img> element in HTML is a placeholder for an image. Or an element may include content as an attribute value. The presence of an empty element in an XML metadata record is indicated by no characters or child elements, not even spaces, between the element's start and close tag. Alternatively, an empty element can be indicated by having '/' as the last character of the start tag (in this case no close tag is required), for example:

```
<yearOfPublication />
```

Attributes

In XML an element may have one or more attributes. Syntactically, XML attributes are included as part of the element start tag. These attributes allow XML authors to associate one or more name-value pairs with the element. The attribute name comes first, followed by the '=' character, followed by the attribute value. The attribute value must be enclosed in quotes; either single or double quotes can be used.

The XML shown in figure 2.1 includes attributes on both `<Author>` elements and on the `<PublicationDate>` element. In XML, attributes are used for various purposes. In some cases they elaborate or refine the meaning of the element. In figure 2.1, Tim Cole is not just an author of the book being described; the presence of the attribute order with a value of 1 (i.e., `order='1'`) presumably tells us that Cole is the first author of the book being described, notwithstanding that his name appears second in the XML metadata record. When processing XML, it is generally bad practice to rely on the order of elements in the XML file. If the order of repeated elements is important, then typically an XML author shows this by adding an appropriate attribute, as illustrated in figure 2.1 with the use of the `order` attribute. (Note that there is nothing special about the name of the attribute; the choice of order here for the attribute name is arbitrary and up to the individual creating the scheme being used.) The attribute included as part of the `<PublicationDate>` element in figure 2.1 serves a different purpose. Here the name-value pair `w3cdtf="2013-04-01"` provides a more machine-friendly formatted version of the human-readable content of this element (`w3cdtf` is a shorthand reference to the W3C Date Time Format).[5]

In XML elements are allowed to have multiple attributes, and these attributes can each serve a different purpose. For example, an attribute could have been used in figure 2.1 to convey full author name information in inverted order, as shown in figure 2.3. Attributes can also be used to switch an element's content model from PCData to Empty, as illustrated in figure 2.4.

There are a few special types of attributes in XML that serve special functions. Among the most important of these in the context of library metadata are `ID`, `IDREF`, and `IDREFS` attributes. The value of an `ID` attribute provides a unique identifier for an element within the scope of an XML document. In

```
<Author order="2" name="Han, Myung-Ja K."> M. J. Han</Author>
<Author order="1" name="Cole, Timothy W.">Tim Cole</Author>
```

Figure 2.3 | **Using attributes to express author metadata in an alternate format**

```
<Author order="2" name="Han, Myung-Ja K." displayName='M.. J. Han' />
<Author order="1" name="Cole, Timothy W." displayName='Tim Cole' />
```

Figure 2.4 | **Attributes used with an Empty content model element**

the following, if the attribute `authID` were defined to be of attribute type `ID`:

```
<Author order="2" authID="a2">M. J. Han</Author>
```

then a consuming application would know that this is the only node in the XML file identified by the string "`a2`." (`ID` type attribute values must be unique within an XML document instance.) Given this certainty, other elements can then use attributes of type `IDREF` or `IDREFS` to reference this `ID` in order to connect one content object (element) to another. This mechanism is particularly useful when serializing information from a relational database in XML. In our illustration, this is useful, for example, when associating an institutional affiliation with the author M. J. Han. Assuming that the attribute `refID` is of attribute type `IDREF`, the following node appearing elsewhere in the XML metadata record tells us M. J. Han's affiliation:

```
<Affiliation refID="a2">University of Illinois at
Urbana Champaign</Affiliation>
```

Note also that attributes that begin with the characters '`xml`' or '`xmlns`' are reserved and may have special meaning; for example, the attribute `xml:lang` is one way to convey the language of text in a content object. (Additional uses of these special attributes are discussed in chapters 4 and 5.)

Special Content: Character Encoding, Entities, and Whitespace

The default character encoding for string content in XML (i.e., PCData) is UTF-8 as defined by the Unicode Consortium. UTF-8 is a way to represent characters in the context of a computer application using 1, 2, 3, or 4 bytes (8, 16, 24, or 32 bits). UTF-8 is a superset of the older American Standard Code for Information Interchange (ASCII) encoding which represented characters with 7 bits (and so supported less than 128 characters). UTF-8 can be used to encode the more than 65,000 characters in the Unicode Basic Multilingual Plane, thus facilitating the inclusion in XML of multilingual content (e.g., diacritics). In theory, UTF-8 can be used to express any of the more than one million characters in all 17 Unicode planes, but some XML applications do not recognize characters beyond the Basic Plane. While it is possible in XML to override the default character encoding, in order to maximize interoperability and content portability, most implementers do not (or if they do, they limit themselves to UTF-16, which is similar to UTF-8 in design and scope and which like UTF-8 is understood by all conformant XML parsers).

Of course, just because a character can be encoded in UTF-8 doesn't mean it is easy to enter from the keyboard. When creating or editing the content of a metadata record, catalogers and metadata authors may choose to include such special characters that are not easily entered from the keyboard using XML character references (also known as character entities). In XML a character reference is a kind of markup that serves as a special character placeholder in PCData content and attribute values. Character references begin with an ampersand character, '&,' and end with a semicolon. All Unicode character references begin '&#' and include a number value which is the Unicode code point for the character desired. These code points are found in the Unicode Code Charts.[6] The number can be in base 10 or base 16 (hexadecimal); in the latter case it is prefixed with the character 'x.' For the copyright symbol (©), the Unicode Code Point is 0169 (decimal) or 00A9 (hexadecimal). A character reference for this symbol could then be inserted as shown below (the options are equivalent). When either of these character references is resolved and the substitution made, the content becomes: © 2013.

```
<copyright>&#0169; 2013</copyright>
or
<copyright>&#x00A9; 2013</copyright>
```

Table 2.1 | **Internal character references built into XML**

CHARACTER REFERENCE	REPLACED BY	CHARACTER NAME
<	<	less than
>	>	greater than
&	&	ampersand
'	‘	apostrophe
"	“	quotation mark

As with HTML, character references are used when including any of five characters that might otherwise be confused with markup delimiters in PCData content or attribute values. Definitions of these special character references, shown in table 2.1, are built into XML.

Though rarely needed, additional character references can be defined and used within individual XML documents. More common, though still rare in library metadata contexts, are internal and external entities. In XML the idea of character references is generalized to internal and external entities. These work in a similar way to character references but are placeholders for more than a single character. As with Unicode character references, all entities start with the '&' character and end with a semicolon, but instead of numbers, alphanumeric mnemonic strings are used. Internal entities are resolved and replaced during XML parsing and are typically used as a shorthand to reference a long string that appears frequently throughout an XML document or a group of XML documents. External entities are placeholders for external content—sometimes an external XML file or fragment, but more often non-textual information, for example, an image.

When serializing metadata in XML, developers and authors need to be cognizant of how XML handles whitespace characters (spaces, tabs, carriage returns, and line feeds). Unless specifically instructed not to do so, XML applications may replace any multicharacter strings of whitespace with a single whitespace character. (The assumption is that line breaks, tabs, and multi-space character sequences are there for convenience or for human readability rather than as a meaningful part of the content.) This is consistent with how HTML handles whitespace; however, there are substantive implications of this behavior in a metadata context, particularly when transforming catalog records from MARC to MARCXML. For example, spaces may be meaningful in some MARC fields; for example, the control field 008 in which the character position is critical to meaning. A special attribute, `xml:space`, may be attached to an element and assigned the value 'preserve' to signal that for a specific element whitespace in content should be preserved. Thus, the following would be one way to ensure the preservation of whitespace:

```
<marc008 xml:space='preserve'>070313s2007    ctua     b
    001 0 eng  </marc008>
```

An element can be declared (discussed in chapter 4) so as to preserve whitespace in content by default (for itself and all its child elements). This is done when defining the element's content model type or by making the xml:space='preserve' attribute name-value pair implicit and fixed. The Library of Congress uses the former option in describing its MARCXML markup scheme, so the xml:space attribute can be left off (illustrated below), as long as the XML serialized metadata record references the Library of Congress MARCXML schema and as long as the XML application is able to retrieve and correctly process the Library of Congress schema.

```
<controlfield tag="008">070313s2007    ctua     b
    001 0 eng  </controlfield>
```

Additional Syntax: Comments, CDATA, and Processing Instructions

XML syntax for elements, attributes, character references, and entities provides ample expressiveness for most XML implementations and applications, but XML also provides additional syntax for inserting comments and special processing instructions into XML metadata records and for handling content that should not be parsed by XML applications.

The start of a comment in XML is delimited by <!-- and the end of an XML comment is delimited by -->. Comments in XML are not parsed by generic XML applications, and strings included in the text of a comment that would normally be recognized as markup or entity references are not treated as such. Comments inserted into an XML document instance should be ignored by generic XML processors and applications. There is no requirement on XML applications to retain comments in their output. The only character sequence that cannot be included in an XML comment is consecutive hyphens, since this is the first part of the sequence of characters used to delineate the end of the comment. As illustrated below, comments are useful as a way to include the version of the locally developed software that created or processed an XML document, or to provide other kinds of human-readable annotations and documentation.

```
<!--$Workfile: Identify.asp $Revision: 7.02 $Date:
8/13/2015 16:21-->
```

Unlike comments, Processing Instructions (PIs) are not meant for human consumption. Rather, PIs are intended for workflow applications and similar specialized uses. All PIs start with the character sequence '<?'. The string immediately following the '?' character is the PITarget and serves as the name or label

by which a processing instruction can be recognized. All PIs are terminated by '?>'. The syntax of what's in between is not parsed by XML applications, and is specific to each PITarget. In general, PIs can safely be ignored by generic XML applications and tools, but unlike comments, XML parsers are required to retain PIs in outputs they generate. Below is an example of a processing instruction for a library cataloging workflow application.

```
<?catModule barcode=30112024718303 bibid=991195
copyNumber=1 ?>
```

Please note that markup starting with '<?xml' is reserved for XML standardization (including possible future standardization). Markup which appears before the root element start tag is known as the XML Prolog. (No content can appear before the root element start tag or after the root element close tag.) The first line of the Prolog is an XML Declaration (if present), which looks like, but is not a processing instruction. The XML Declaration if present must appear at the very beginning of every XML document instance. The XML Declaration is optional for XML version 1.0, but is required for XML version 1.1.

```
<?xml version='1.1' encoding='UTF-8' standalone='no' ?>
```

A special PI can be used to associate a stylesheet with an XML file. This xml-stylesheet PI should appear in the XML Prolog, below the XML Declaration but before the root element start tag. The following xml-stylesheet PI instructs rendering agents to use a CSS stylesheet file named default.css to format the XML that follows.

```
<?xml-stylesheet type="text/css" href="default.css"
title="Default style"?>
```

As will be illustrated in chapter 4, other markup in the XML Prolog is available to associate files used for validating XML document instances, including XML metadata records.

As alluded to above, most content in an XML document instance is meant to be parsed by XML applications—hence the term "parsed character data," abbreviated as PCData. CDATA delimiters allow XML authors to include character data (strings of characters) that are not parsed. The start of a segment of CDATA is delimited by the string '`<! [CDATA[`'. Any text encountered by an XML parser after this delimiter—even text that would normally be recognized as markup (e.g., `<` and `&`), or would be subject to normalization (e.g., collapsing consecutive whitespace characters into a single space), or would be recognized as a character reference or an entity (e.g., `©`)—is left unchanged and is not treated as markup. This behavior continues until the XML parser encounters the CDATA end-delimiter, '`]]>`'. The only character sequence that cannot be included in a CDATA segment is the string '`]]>`', since this is the sequence of characters used to delineate the end of a CDATA segment. While some XML authors do use CDATA for embedding snippets of HTML or XML, for documentation, or as part of a tutorial, CDATA is not much encountered in library XML applications. For binary data (e.g., image data), external entities should be preferred to CDATA.

Well-Formed XML vs. Valid XML

An XML document instance that conforms to the syntax rules summarized above is termed "well-formed" in XML parlance. As long as it has a single root element, an element hierarchy without overlaps, a close tag for every open tag, quote marks around every attribute value, and so on, an XML parser will be able to process the file. For many use cases, this is enough. Web browsers, for example, are primarily presentation and hyperlinking applications; for the most part, they do not need to know whether or not the XML metadata record requested conforms to the semantics and grammar of a particular metadata standard in order to display the record. As long as the XML metadata record is well-formed, these kinds of applications will process it.

For other use cases, however, XML validation against a defined scheme—one that specifies content object labels, content models, and the structure of the content object hierarchy—can be valuable. Consider that a metadata librarian could misspell an element name. As long as he or she did so consistently in both the start-tag and end-tag, the XML document instance could still be well-formed. But relying on well-formedness alone, a computer application written to recognize specific labels would not recognize the misspelled element, and so would not process the XML metadata correctly. Or an essential element might inadvertently be left out of a metadata record. Or a cataloger might accidentally introduce an inconsistency in the structure of a record.

To help avoid such problems, the W3C XML Recommendation adds to the idea of well-formedness the concept of XML document instance validity. To support validation, metadata semantic and structural constraints for a specific class of XML document instances or a specific XML application (e.g., a specific metadata format) are described, either in an XML Document Type Definition (DTD) or an XML schema document. The DTD or schema is then referenced in the XML Prolog or in the root element start tag. A well-formed XML document instance that also conforms to the constraints of a DTD or schema is a valid XML document instance. XML applications and services that support use cases requiring document validity rely on validating XML parsers that can read schemas and/or DTDs.

XML metadata applications that only require well-formedness are easier and require less overhead and less resources overall. Well-formedness is sufficient for rapid prototyping projects and makes sense for small-team, short-duration, ad-hoc metadata projects dealing with mostly simple, homogeneous metadata records, especially if there are minimal expectations for reuse or retention of the XML metadata records. XML validation is more appropriate for longer-term, larger-scale, collaborative projects involving multiple, widely dispersed metadata librarians who are likely working together over multiple years. XML validation facilitates interoperability and supports more robust quality assurance. The syntax rules introduced in this chapter are sufficient to create well-formed XML. Chapter 4 introduces the World Wide Web Consortium's XML Schema Definition Language and illustrates how it is used to validate XML metadata.

Notes

1. S. J. DeRose, D. G. Durand, E. Mylonas, and A. H. Renear, "What Is Text, Really?" *Journal of Computing in Higher Education* 1, no. 2 (December 1990): 3–26, doi:10.1007/BF02941632.
2. Tim Bray, Jean Paoli, C. M. Sperberg-McQueen, Eve Maler, and François Yergeau, eds., *W3C Recommendation: Extensible Markup Language (XML) 1.0,* 5th edition (Cambridge, MA: Massachusetts Institute of Technology, 2008), www.w3.org/TR/xml/.
3. UTF stands for Unicode Transformation Format. UTF-8, UTF-16, and UTF-32 are variants promulgated by the Unicode Consortium, Mountain View, CA. For more information, see www.w3.org/International/articles/definitions-characters/, www.unicode.org/versions/Unicode7.0.0/ch03.pdf#G28070, www.unicode.org/reports/tr42/.
4. Library of Congress Network Development and MARC Standards Office, *MARC 21 Specifications for Record Structure, Character Sets, and Exchange Media: Character Sets and Encoding Options* (Washington, DC: Library of Congress, 2007), www.loc.gov/marc/specifications/speccharintro.html.
5. Misha Wolf and Charles Wicksteed, *W3C Note: Date and Time Formats* (Cambridge, MA: Massachusetts Institute of Technology, 1997), www.w3.org/TR/NOTE-datetime.
6. Unicode Consortium, *Unicode 9.0 Character Code Charts* (Mountain View, CA: Unicode Consortium, 2016), www.unicode.org/charts/.

LIBRARY METADATA IN XML

As information technologies have advanced rapidly, cataloging and metadata practices at memory institutions also have evolved to create records that are more readable and processable by machines and more readily reusable by others, especially metadata aggregators and service providers. The goal is to make library and cultural heritage resources more visible and discoverable. Instead of relying solely on MAchine Readable Cataloging (MARC) metadata in binary format (as originally designed for interchange via magnetic tape), libraries have begun migrating to (or at least managing in parallel) MARC catalog records in XML format.[1] XML makes it easier to process and share catalog records. To make their metadata more shareable still, and to better describe nonbook materials that require different descriptive attributes than traditional print resources, libraries and other cultural heritage institutions also have begun making use of other XML-based metadata formats, including Dublin Core, the Metadata Object Description Schema (MODS), Encoded Archival Description (EAD), and so on (see chapter 12).[2] Additionally, in order to fulfill emerging needs that require new or modified metadata schemas, libraries are developing XML-based metadata application profiles that allow the use of semantics from multiple different schemas simultaneously.[3] This chapter will illustrate the use of three XML-based metadata standards (MARC, Dublin Core, and MODS) that are among the most used in libraries, and it will discuss aspects of schema design that libraries need to consider when choosing a metadata standard as new needs arise, including factors such as the systems where metadata is created and stored, functional requirements, and granularity of description.

MARCXML

MARC 21, the current edition of the MARC standard for cataloging (as maintained by the Library of Congress), was introduced in 1997, the result of harmonizing and aligning the *USMARC Format for Bibliographic Data* and the *Canadian MARC Communication Format for Bibliographic Data.* MARCXML is the de facto standard for serializing MARC 21 catalog records in XML. The XML schema for MARCXML was introduced in 2002. Today MARCXML is widely used for exchanging library data between institutions and to facilitate transforming MARC records to other metadata standards, because MARCXML is easier to read, enhance, and analyze than binary MARC. When individual libraries began collaborating with Google on mass digitization efforts in 2004, each participating library submitted its whole catalog (including holdings and individual item descriptive metadata) in MARCXML format to Google so that Google could analyze the collections and items held in each library and identify uniquely held items. Similarly, the HathiTrust Digital Library (https://www.hathitrust.org/) also asks contributing libraries to submit catalog records in MARCXML format (also enriched with item descriptive metadata) whenever they wish to add new contents into the HathiTrust.

Most library online public access catalog (OPAC) applications still ingest binary MARC-formatted catalog records. They use these MARC records to build indexes and internal data structures that are then used to generate OPAC catalog record displays such as illustrated in figure 3.1 (note the variant spelling as accurately transcribed from the item's 1860 title page). However, many of these same library systems also provide alternative views in their interfaces that reveal the underlying MARC structure of catalog records and options in their application program interfaces (APIs) that provide access to the record in MARCXML.

Figure 3.2 shows an alternate "staff" view of the catalog record presented in figure 3.1, exposing the MARC structure of the record. Stimulated by a continuing interest in interoperability, the option to retrieve from library systems

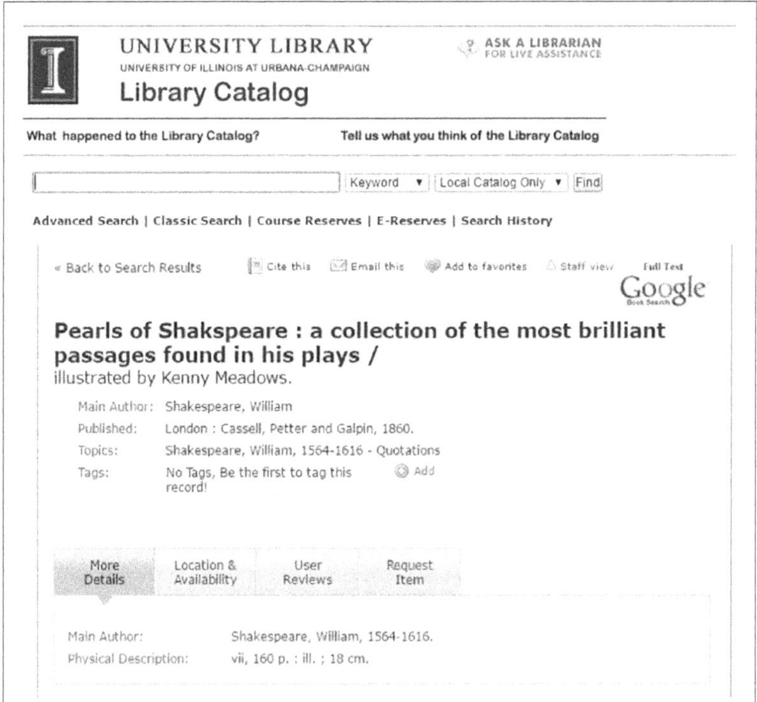

Figure 3.1 | **OPAC display of a library catalog record describing *Pearls of Shakspeare* [sic]**

a MARCXML serialization of library catalog records is becoming ubiquitous. Relying on attributes to carry much of the intellectual semantics of a catalog record, MARCXML defines only a few elements: two top-level elements (`<collection>`, `<record>`), `<leader>`, `<controlfield>`, `<datafield>`, and `<subfield>`.

Rather than create a uniquely named element for each potential subfield code and datafield (e.g., main entry, title statement, etc.), XML attributes are used to express MARC tag, subfield code, and indicator values. The resulting intellectual mapping of binary MARC to MARCXML is straightforward, as illustrated in table 3.1. A major benefit of MARCXML is that it allows libraries to retain all information present in the original binary MARC in MARCXML format. Since MARCXML supports the same structure and semantics as binary MARC 21, libraries don't need to worry about information loss, which often happens in the mapping and transformation process from one metadata standard to another.

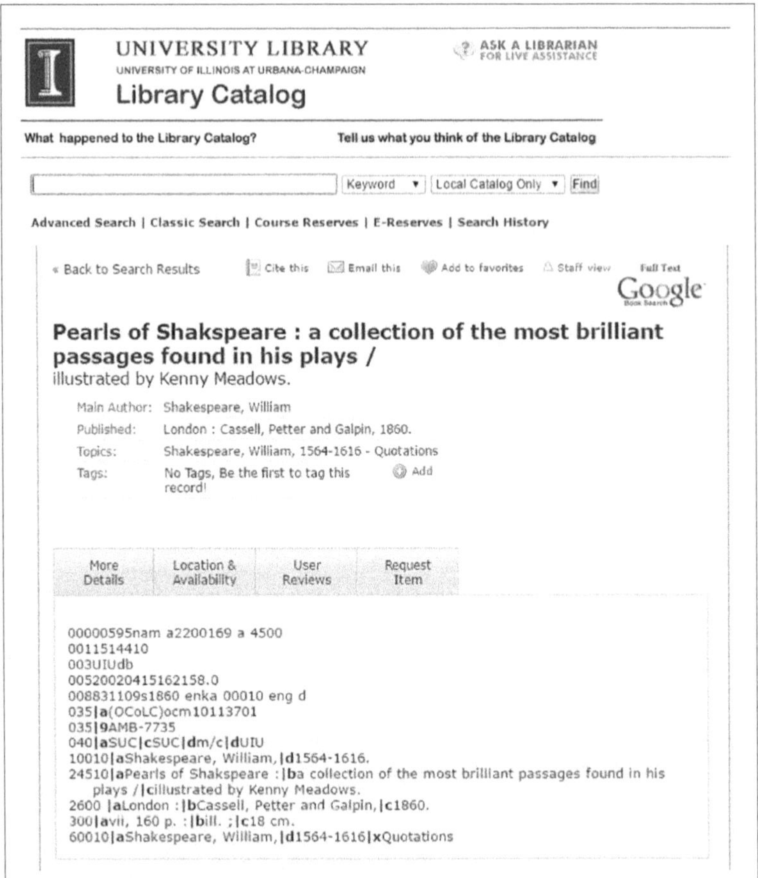

Figure 3.2 | **"Staff" (i.e., MARC) view of catalog record describing *Pearls of Shakspeare* [sic]**

Additionally, because the MARCXML schema only defines a limited number of elements and attributes, it is relatively easy to define and use 9XX datafields and subfields to extend MARC to support local needs. For example, the HathiTrust defines the datafield 955 as a place for local information about each item submitted.[4] Before submitting the item and its MARCXML record to the HathiTrust, the contributing institution populates datafield 955 with the item's local identifier (e.g., bar code) and volume chronology/enumeration information, as illustrated in table 3.2.

Interestingly, datafield 955 is also used when submitting metadata to Google, but for different purposes (as illustrated in table 3.3). This demonstrates how easily MARCXML can support the use of 9XX extensions to meet local needs.

Table 3.1 | **Illustrating how MARC datafields, indicators, and subfields map to MARCXML**

MARC DATAFIELDS AND SUBFIELDS	MARC XML SERIALIZATION EXAMPLE
datafield 100: indicators: 10 $a: Shakespeare, William, $d: 1564-1616.	*<datafield tag=*“100”*ind1=*“1” *ind2=*“0”> <*subfield code=*“a”>Shakespeare, William, </*subfield*> <*subfield code=*“d”>1564-1616.</*subfield*> </*datafield*>
datafield 245: indicators: 10 $a: Pearls of Shakespeare : $b: a collection of the most brilliant passages found in his plays / $c: illustrated by Kenny Meadows.	<*datafield tag=*“245” *ind1=*“1” *ind2=*“0”> <*subfield code=*“a”>Pearls of Shakespeare :</*subfield*> <*subfield code=*“b”>a collection of the most brilliant passages found in his plays /</*subfield*> <*subfield code=*“c”>illustrated by Kenny Meadows.</*subfield*> </*datafield*>

Table 3.2 | **MARC datafield 955 as defined by HathiTrust for locally digitized items**

MARC DATAFIELD AND SUBFIELDS	MARC XML SERIALIZATION EXAMPLE
datafield: 955 $b: local ID $v: vol. information	<*datafield tag=*“955” *ind1=*“ ” *ind2=*“ ”> <*subfield code=*“b”>30112000013836</*subfield*> <*subfield code=*“v”>1988</*subfield*> </*datafield*>

Table 3.3 | **MARC datafield 955 as defined by Google**

MARC XML SERIALIZATION	MARC XML SERIALIZATION EXAMPLE
datafield: 955 $a: institution code $b: unique item ID $c: item record ID $d: location $e: classification no. $f: copy no. $g: mono/serials $v: vol. information	<*datafield tag=*“955” *ind1=*“ ” *ind2=*“ ”> <*subfield code=*“a”>UIU</*subfield*> <*subfield code=*“b”>30112000013836</*subfield*> <*subfield code=*“c”>3153716</*subfield*> <*subfield code=*“d”>Oak Street [req only]</*subfield*> <*subfield code=*“e”>330.97291 C8923</*subfield*> <*subfield code=*“f”>1</*subfield*> <*subfield code=*“g”>as</*subfield*> <*subfield code=*“v”>1988</*subfield*> </*datafield*>

While there have been many discussions regarding the future of bibliographic control in the library, many of which have touched on alternatives to MARC-based library metadata that are more suitable for use in a linked data and semantic web environment, MARC 21 and MARCXML will continue to be used in the library for some time to come for the following reasons:

- Flexibility for using library metadata that is created with a community-shared content standard (AACR 2 or RDA) in MARC 21 format5
- The option currently being explored of using subfield $0 (Authority record control number or standard number) as a place for a Uniform Resources Identifier (URI) corresponding to the string value added in subfields $a or $t of datafields 1XX, 7XX, and 6XX
- The large installed base of library systems that rely on MARC and the large legacy collections of library catalog data maintained by libraries in MARC 21 format—MARC remains the primary schema for metadata used by integrated library systems

DUBLIN CORE

Dublin Core was originally developed for describing web pages. It was designed so that Dublin Core metadata could be easily embedded into HTML web pages. It is now used for describing digital resources in many different formats, including images, text, audiovisual resources, and maps. Dublin Core is included as a default metadata standard in several digital asset management systems, including CONTENTdm (www.contentdm.org/), DSpace (www.dspace.org/), and Omeka (https://omeka.org/). Dublin Core is also required as a minimum metadata standard for the Open Archives Initiative—Protocol for Metadata Harvesting (OAI-PMH) when sharing digital resource metadata with service providers.[6] A large portion of metadata contributed to the Digital Public Library of America (DPLA; https://dp.la/) is in Dublin Core because much of it has been harvested using OAI-PMH and describes digital items housed in digital asset management systems that use Dublin Core.

Known as an everyman's metadata, "simple" Dublin Core, that is, version 1.1 of the Dublin Core Metadata Element Set (http://dublincore.org/documents/dces/) consists of fifteen elements, which have since been extended with qualifying terms (additional elements in XML) that refine the semantics of simple Dublin Core elements and additional elements that are required for describing more granular/complex types of information than originally considered.

Table 3.4 | **Dublin Core Terms allows type and language attributes for values of subject**

Simple Dublin Core	*<dc:subject>* XML (Document markup language)*</dc:subject>*
Qualified Dublin Core	*<dcterms:subject xsi:type=*"dcterms:LCSH"*xml:lang=*"en"> XML (Document markup language)*</dcterms:subject>*

(Collectively, these extensions and refinements are known as "qualified" Dublin Core, or more recently Dublin Core Metadata Initiative Metadata Terms or simply Dublin Core Terms, http://dublincore.org/documents/dcmi-terms/.) While the simple Dublin Core schema defines elements only, the Dublin Core Terms vocabulary also defines encoding schemes and syntax encoding schemes that can help ensure consistent metadata quality. As illustrated above, when using the subject element in simple Dublin Core, there is no way to know from which vocabulary the value came, that is, on which controlled vocabulary the metadata author is relying. This could be important information when doing reconciliation work; for example, to identify what linked data sources the system should use to find matching URIs. Table 3.4 shows one way subject may be serialized differently in XML for simple and qualified Dublin Core. As illustrated, using this serialization approach, Dublin Core Terms allows the addition of attributes that specify the subject authority used and the language of the value of the subject element.

Every element in Dublin Core is repeatable, and none of them are required. The simplicity, as well as the broad and general design of Dublin Core semantics (elements), make the metadata standard popular. Unlike MARCXML, Dublin Core does not have a shared content standard that is required or used when creating metadata. Because of this, it is considered best practice to have complete documentation or a fully described application profile explaining how each Dublin Core element is used in a specific project or collection.

METADATA OBJECT DESCRIPTION SCHEMA (MODS)

MODS is known as a simplified and human-readable version of MARC. Instead of the numerically coded datafield tag and subfield code approach used in MARCXML, it has a set of human-readable elements and attributes. Since MODS has the same hierarchical structure and rich semantics, but is relatively easier (for humans) to read and edit than MARC, a growing number of institutions are using MODS as their descriptive metadata standard for

```
<name
   type="personal"
   authorityURI="http://viaf.org"
   valueURI=" http://viaf.org/viaf/96994048">
  <namePart>Shakespeare, William</namePart>
  <namePart type="date">1564-1616</namePart>
</name>
```

Figure 3.3 | **MODS has attributes for associating URIs with string values (i.e., element content)**

digital repositories, and some are transforming their MARC-formatted bibliographic data to MODS. Similar to MARCXML, the MODS XML schema allows both `<collection>` and `<record>` as root elements. In contrast to MARCXML, the MODS schema defines a set of top-level elements, each having a set of sub-elements and attributes. Among the common attributes across elements are `authority`, `authorityURI`, and `valueURI`. This means that elements within MODS records can include URIs in addition to string values for transitioning to linked data (as illustrated in figure 3.3).

A significant difference between MARC and MODS is that MODS can include holdings and item-level information in a record containing bibliographic information by using the top-level element `<location>` and (for example) the associated sub-elements `<holdingSimple>` and `<copyInformation>`, which are not available in the MARC 21 Format for Bibliographic Data. In MODS version 3.6, the MODS Editorial board added a new sub-element `<itemIdentifier>` under the element `<copyInformation>`. Using the `type` attribute of this new element, an institution can specify the nature of the item-level identifier recorded. This allows catalogers to record item information in greater detail, as illustrated in figure 3.4.

MODS is also used for describing digital resources, collections, and archives, in part because the `<location>` element has child nodes (e.g., `<url>`, `<physicalLocation>`) for expressing from where resources may be obtained. Additionally, the element `<relatedItem>` can describe a related resource using the complete semantics of MODS, which is useful for describing resources embedded within an archives hierarchical structure or which have complex series information and relationships that need to be expressed. Figure 3.5 illustrates the use of the `<relatedItem>` element.

MODS has MARCXML's hierarchical structure and rich semantics with well-defined meanings that are human-readable. On top of this, MODS

```
<location>
   <physicalLocation displayLabel="InstitutionCode">IU</
physicalLocation>
   <holdingSimple>
      <copyInformation>
        <subLocation>Social Sciences, Health, and Education</
subLocation>
        <shelfLocator>370.7206 Ie1</shelfLocator>
        <note displayLabel="Copy Number">1</note>
        <itemIdentifier type="Barcode">30112110468615</note>
        <enumerationAndChronology>v.2</enumerationAndChronology>
      </copyInformation>
   </holdingSimple>
</location>
```

Figure 3.4 | **Illustrating the use of the location, holdingSimple and copyInformation elements**

```
<relatedItem>
   <titleInfo>
     <title>Dynamic physical education for secondary school
students, 7th ed</title>
   </titleInfo>
   <name type="personal">
     <namePart>Darst, Paul W.</namePart>
   </name>
</relatedItem>
```

Figure 3.5 | **The MODS relatedItem element can contain a complete MODS description**

serialized as XML is well-suited to the task as libraries move forward into the era of the semantic web and linked open data.

HOW LIBRARIES SELECT METADATA STANDARDS

In her graphical view of library metadata standards, *Seeing Standard: A Visualization of the Metadata Universe*, Jenn Riley enumerates more than 100 metadata standards and associated content standards.[7] And this was back in 2010; there are many more metadata standards in use today. In order to choose the best metadata standards for a particular purpose, libraries have to look at several issues and considerations before making decisions.

1. *Systems used for metadata*

   There are many digital asset management systems out there, both open source and proprietary systems. None support all available metadata standards. As mentioned earlier, CONTENTdm, DSpace, and Omeka support at least simple Dublin Core as their default metadata standard. These systems provide options for local extensions to Dublin Core, but if these are utilized, exporting the resulting metadata records to service providers that are expecting simple Dublin Core may be problematic. Most integrated library systems support only MARC-format metadata. Open source or locally developed systems may provide better options for customizable metadata. However, the selection of a metadata standard can and should be supported by the system chosen and should be based in large part on what delivery, access, and preservation services the library requires.

2. *Functional requirements for bibliographic records*

   In addition to considering which metadata standard to choose based on the system to be implemented, a library must assess the scope and functionality of the services that can be provided to library users based on metadata design. If the library will provide a keyword search over full content service, then the metadata standard may not need to support highly granular levels of description. However, if the library will provide an advanced search service or faceted browsing services based on specific, granular descriptive attributes, for example by using first name or last name, the metadata scheme must provide the semantics needed to support this functionality. Interestingly, although MARC has more than 1,900 fields, first name and last name are not recorded separately, that is, first names and last names are separable only by making assumptions about format and punctuation. In this respect MODS is better. Also, when describing different types of names, catalogers or metadata professionals implementing both MARC and MODS differentiate between personal, corporate, and meeting names. In MARC these differences result in the name being located in datafields with different tags (e.g., 100, 110, 111). In MODS, these differences can be negotiated by examining the top-level name element's type attribute values. Unfortunately, Dublin Core does not have semantics to support the granularity of name parts or different types of names. Table 3.5 shows how MARC, Dublin Core, and MODS yield different results when

Table 3.5 | **Creator name is described differently in MARC, Dublin Core, and MODS**

MARCXML	<datafield tag=“100” ind1=“1” ind2=“ ”> <subfield code=“a”>Shakespeare, William 1564-1616</subfield> <subfield code=“d”>1564-1616</subfield> </datafield>
Dublin Core	<dc:creator>Shakespeare, William 1564-1616</dc:creator>
MODS	<name type=“personal” authorityURI=“http://viaf.org” valueURI=“http://viaf.org/viaf/96994048”> <namePart type=“family”>Shakespeare</namePart> <namePart type=“given”>William</namePart> <namePart type=“date”>1564-1616</namePart> <role> <roleTerm type=“text” authority=“marcrelator”>author</roleTerm> <roleTerm type=“code” authority=“marcrelator”>aut</roleTerm> </role> </name>

describing the same name in the role of creator. Names with other roles than creator are also described differently. As illustrated in table 3.6, both MARCXML and MODS have specific subfields (MARCXML) and attributes (MODS) for roles. Catalogers and metadata specialists use controlled vocabularies to describe role information. By contrast, Dublin Core has only the contributor element for all roles other than creator. Due to this limitation, role information in Dublin Core is often added using parentheses to the value of the `<contributor>` element, but this is convention only and is not universally followed.

3. ***Who will create the metadata?***

   The selection of metadata standards should take into account who will be the metadata creator as well. If an institution or a project has professional catalogers who understand content standards and controlled vocabularies, or have deep subject knowledge, the chosen metadata standard can be more descriptive, with highly granular levels of semantics. But if it will be undergraduate students creating the metadata, the metadata standard should be something that is easy to use by novices, unless there is a tool that will guide the user and help ensure proper metadata input. The University of Illinois at Urbana-Champaign Library developed a

Table 3.6 | **MARCXML and MODS can describe role while Dublin Core cannot**

MARCXML	*<datafield tag=“700” ind1=“1” ind2=“ ”>* *<subfield code=“a”>*Shakespeare, William 1564-1616*</subfield>* *<subfield code=*“d”>1564-1616*</subfield>* *<subfield code=*“e”>illustrator*</subfield>* *</datafield>*
Dublin Core	*<dc:contributor>*Shakespeare, William 1564-1616*</dc:contributor>* *or* *<dc:contributor>*Shakespeare, William 1564-1616 (illustrator)*</dc:contributor>*
MODS	*<name* *type=*“personal” *authorityURI=*“http://viaf.org” *valueURI=*“http://viaf.org/viaf/96994048”> *<namePart>*Shakespeare, William*</namePart>* *<namePart type=*“date”>1564-1616*</namePart>* *<role>* *<roleTerm type=*“text” *authority=*“marcrelator”>illustrator*</roleTerm>* *<roleTerm type=*“code” authority=“marcrelator”*>ilu</roleTerm>* *</role>* *</name>*

metadata creation tool for student assistants called Metadata Maker (http://quest.library.illinois.edu/marcmaker/). Although the tool has a simple interface for people who do not have cataloging experience or metadata knowledge, it can create metadata conforming to three different standards, MARCXML (and MARC21), MODS, and schema .org embedded in HTML.

4. *Time line*

   Time is another factor that should be considered when selecting a metadata standard for a project. If there is a clear deadline for all metadata to be created, then metadata may not be able to be created in granular levels with specific controlled vocabularies. Instead, the metadata standard should be something that is simple but captures the essential characteristics of the collection and items. If a consistent metadata plan is set and followed, records later can be transformed into other standards using EXtensible Stylesheet Language Transformation (XSLT) with an opportunity for enrichment. Chapter 6 discusses and illustrates how XSLT can help catalog and metadata workflows.

In addition to these four considerations, cataloging and metadata professionals should also consider overall project workflow design. Not many libraries create metadata in XML format from scratch using an XML editor. In many cases, XML-based metadata is initially created in some kind of template (spreadsheets are often used) and then transformed into XML metadata. In such a case, decisions on metadata standards should take into account the characteristics of resources and users' needs, and finally a well-designed metadata workflow.

Notes

1. Library of Congress Network Development and MARC Standards Office, *MARC Standards,* 2017, https://www.loc.gov/marc/; Library of Congress Network Development and MARC Standards Office, *MARCXML: MARC 21 XML Schema, Official Web Site,* 2016, https://www.loc.gov/standards/marcxml/.
2. DCMI Usage Board, *DCMI Metadata Terms,* 2012, http://dublincore.org/documents/dcmi-terms/; Library of Congress Network Development and MARC Standards Office, *MODS: Metadata Object Description Schema, Official Web Site,* 2017, www.loc.gov/standards/mods/; Library of Congress Network Development and MARC Standards Office, *<ead>: Encoded Archival Description, Official Site,* 2017, www.loc.gov/ead/.
3. Rachel Heery and Manjula Patel, "Application Profiles: Mixing and Matching Metadata Schemas," *Ariadne* 25 (September 24, 2000), www.ariadne.ac.uk/issue25/app-profiles.
4. HathiTrust Digital Library, *Bibliographic Metadata Submission: Overview of Bibliographic Metadata Submission Process,* https://www.hathitrust.org/bib_data_submission.
5. American Library Association, Canadian Library Association, and Chartered Institute of Library and Information Professionals, *Anglo-American Cataloguing Rules, Second Edition,* 2002 Revision, 2005, www.aacr2.org/; Acquisitions and Bibliographic Access Directorate, Library of Congress, *Resource Description and Access (RDA): Information and Resources in Preparation for RDA,* https://www.loc.gov/aba/rda/.
6. Open Archives Initiative, *Open Archives Initiative Protocol for Metadata Harvesting,* https://www.openarchives.org/pmh/.
7. Jenn Riley, *Seeing Standard: A Visualization of the Metadata Universe,* 2010, http://jennriley.com/metadatamap/.

XML VALIDATION USING SCHEMAS

The flexibility of XML as a framework for conveying structured information like library metadata is one of its greatest strengths. However, most applications used by libraries to organize, describe, inventory, and index licensed materials and tangible content holdings require metadata records that are consistently structured and follow community-standard metadata models. Coding efficiency suffers in the absence of structural consistency and semantic standardization, especially when metadata records are shared across multiple departments or institutions or are expected to be maintained and reused beyond the current project. This begs the question, does XML offer an efficient way that digital library architects can ensure the consistency and interoperability of metadata records? Specifically, is there an automated way to

- Check record structure against an XML-compatible data model, that is, recognize optional, contingent, and required elements and verify that data model rules, hierarchy requirements, and similar constraints have been satisfied record by record;
- Confirm conformance to data type constraints for XML element content and attribute values;

- Confirm conformance to other constraints on XML elements and attributes?

The answer is mostly yes, though in XML the ability to check values beyond data type is limited. The key for enabling this functionality, as alluded to at the end of chapter 2, begins by differentiating between well-formed XML and valid XML. A document instance that conforms to the fixed and invariant syntax of XML is termed well-formed. Well-formed XML which also conforms to the constraints of a Document Type Definition (DTD) or an XML schema is valid XML with respect to that DTD or schema. XML schemas are much more widely used today than XML DTDs, so in this chapter we focus on the creation and use of XML schemas.

BENEFITS AND LIMITATIONS OF VALID XML

In libraries at least, the World Wide Web Consortium's XML Schema Definition Language Recommendation is the most widely implemented XML schema format.[1] Before exploring the semantics of the XML Schema Definition Language, it is useful to summarize briefly the tradeoffs of relying on valid XML (as opposed to building an XML application that is reliant only on well-formed XML). Requiring XML validation is more rigorous, but it is also more work. Schema documents require time and effort to create and maintain, but they are a way to provide useful, structured views of application-specific grammars that build on the foundational rules and syntax of the XML meta-markup model of information.

In a library context, XML schemas are a good approach for larger metadata or cataloging projects being carried out by teams of people (as opposed to a single individual) because schemas can help enforce a measure of cross-cataloger consistency. For this same reason, valid XML is also better for resource description projects that will take multiple years to complete, need to be maintained for an extended period, have the potential for reuse in additional contexts, and/or involve a complex metadata design featuring a lengthy list of optional and contingent fields and properties. XML schemas allow system architects to unambiguously differentiate between required and optional elements and to define required descriptive granularity. XML schemas help align and make explicit the expectations of both metadata authors and metadata consumers (including computer programs). As compared to DTDs, XML schemas are themselves well-formed and valid XML document instances, obviating the need to learn a different syntax for writing validation constraints.

Through the use of namespaces (see below), XML schemas are optimized for modular development and extension over time; this can facilitate how libraries work with multiple descriptive standards and metadata application profiles. In most library metadata and cataloging project contexts, these are all attributes that are conducive to writing efficient processing algorithms and workflows.

Nevertheless, schemas are not a panacea. XML schemas can only validate metadata record structural design and a limited range of data and value constraints. XML schemas define the property names and other labels allowed for a set of metadata records, but they do not define the semantic meaning of these names and labels. Documentation of what is meant when using field names like mainEntry, title, or author in a specific context (e.g., a library metadata project) must be provided separately, and many rules for validating values (e.g., formatting rules for the full range of possible author names) must be left to domain-specific tools and/or human vetting. Still, XML validation can be an important part of a project's quality assurance strategy.

NAMESPACES AS USED IN XML SCHEMAS AND DOCUMENT INSTANCES

The model for namespaces in XML is described in a W3C Recommendation designed to facilitate semantic interoperability and modular grammar design.[2] The XML namespaces model builds on an approach borrowed from the computer science domain. Unlike most other standards in the XML family of W3C recommendations, the namespace model is not an approach inherited from Standard Generalized Markup Languages. Namespaces enable XML schemas to be authored modularly and extended over time.

In computer programming, namespaces are used as a way to bind together a logical grouping of entity identifiers (e.g., variable names). In the abstract, a namespace is said to contain the names in the logical grouping. In practice, a namespace can be thought of as a modifier that qualifies each of a set of names as belonging to a specific class; for example, those belonging to a specific subroutine module. The goal is to facilitate modularity and reuse. In the modular design of computer programs, namespaces provide a way to keep labels and variable names borrowed from one subroutine in one application from being confused with similar labels and variable names as used in another subroutine borrowed from a different application. Namespaces disambiguate. This ability to avoid ambiguity improves efficiency, and it facilitates reuse and the evolution of naming conventions.

In a cataloging context, potential element name collisions spanning the boundaries of XML metadata grammars can be avoided through the use of XML namespaces. For example, both the Metadata Object Description Schema (MODS) and simple Dublin Core include a subject element. In both standards, the value of this element conveys what the resource is about. In MODS, the semantic meaning of the element subject is broad and child elements are used to distinguish topical subjects from geographic subjects from temporal subjects. In simple Dublin Core, on the other hand, the meaning of the element subject is focused exclusively on topical subjects (encompassing proper names and occupations when used as topical subjects). Simple Dublin Core provides a different element, coverage, to describe the spatial and temporal scope of a resource. Though overlapping, the exact meanings of MODS subject and simple Dublin Core subject are different, and these differences must be recognized by metadata applications dealing with both grammars simultaneously. In practice, this is best achieved through the use of XML namespaces.

Syntactically, XML namespaces are uniquely and persistently identified by URIs (Uniform Resource Identifiers). Namespaces used in an XML document instance are declared through attributes which begin '`xmlns`.' These attributes can appear on the root element or on almost any subsequent element in the XML document tree. (There are rules beyond the range of this discussion for how the scope of a namespace declaration within a document is to be understood depending on where in the document the attribute appears.) The URI for the namespace containing MODS semantics is www.loc.gov/mods/v3. Accordingly, the opening tag of a MODS metadata record root element (e.g., `<mods>`) might appear as illustrated in figure 4.1.

XML applications understand that the default namespace (`xmlns` attribute) for this XML document instance is the MODS namespace. All elements and attributes appearing in this document instance are therefore assumed to be in the MODS namespace unless preceded by an explicit prefix bound to another namespace. As indicated by the presence of the `xmlns:xsi` attribute, one other namespace is declared in this root element. This additional namespace declaration tells an XML application that when elements or attributes from the XML Schema Instance namespace appear in this document, their names will be prefixed by the string '`xsi:`'. The other two attributes on this root element indicate the version of the MODS schema used and associate the URL of the MODS XML schema definition document (.xsd file extension) with the URI of the MODS namespace.

To encourage the use of XML schemas, the semantics of the XML Schema Definition Language itself are contained in a namespace. Its URI is: www

```
<mods version="3.6"
   xmlns="http://www.loc.gov/mods/v3"
   xmlns:xsi="http://www.w3.org/2001/XMLSchema-instance"
   xsi:schemaLocation="http://www.loc.gov/mods/v3 http://www.loc.gov/
standards/mods/v3/mods-3-6.xsd" >
```

Figure 4.1 | **The opening tag of a MODS record root element (mods) with namespace declarations**

```
<xs:schema
   xmlns="http://www.loc.gov/mods/v3"
   xmlns:xs="http://www.w3.org/2001/XMLSchema"
   xmlns:xlink="http://www.w3.org/1999/xlink"
   targetNamespace="http://www.loc.gov/mods/v3"
   elementFormDefault="qualified"
   attributeFormDefault="unqualified" >
```

Figure 4.2 | **The opening tag of the root element (xs:schema) of the MODS Schema**

.w3.org/2001/XMLSchema. The root element of a schema written in the XML Schema Definition Language will reference this URI in a namespace attribute (e.g., `xmlns:xs`). For example, figure 4.2 shows the opening tag of the root element (`<xs:schema>`) of the MODS schema definition document (version 3.6). The `targetNamespace`, `elementFormDefault`, and `attributeFormDefault` attributes are Schema Definition language-specific and set options for how XML parsers are to interpret the element and attribute declarations included in this schema definition document instance.

DECLARING ELEMENTS, ATTRIBUTES, AND TYPES IN AN XML SCHEMA

The semantics of the W3C's XML Schema Definition language allow a schema author to use XML syntax to declare an element or attribute, name it, associate a data type with it, give it a default value, and define whether it is required or optional. When declaring an element, schema authors can declare whether the element is repeatable or not and can define the content model of the element (including definitions of optional or required attributes). These kinds of rules are expressed in a schema by using XML elements and attributes in the schema definition namespace and by reference, for example, to definitions elsewhere in the schema file, definitions in other existing schema modules, or definitions of predefined primitive and derived data types built into the XML Schema Definition Language. The following single line of XML illustrates one of the simplest ways to declare a new optional (value of `minOccurs` attribute is 0), repeatable (value of `maxOccurs` is unbounded) element named `<date>` (value of `name` is `date`).

```
<xs:element name="date" type="xs:date" minOccurs="0"
maxOccurs="unbounded"/>
```

This element declaration also says that the value of the element `<date>` must be a date, as defined by the XML Schema Definition Language (value of `type` is `xs:date`). Note that this date data type mandates strictly formatted dates, expressing all of the year, month, and day (e.g., 2002–01–24). For some collections this precision of date may not be available for all items, in which case a more flexible date field might be called for; for example, data type `xs:string` would allow "`circa 1650`" as a value.

Attributes are declared in a similar fashion.

```
<xs:attribute name="order" type="xs:integer"
default="0" />
```

In this case, the attribute's name is order (value of `name` attribute is `order`), it is of built-in type integer (value of `type` is `xs:integer`), and if absent in the document instance, its value can be assumed to be 0 (value of `default` is `0`).

As alluded to above, in order to facilitate declaring an element's or attribute's data type, the W3C's XML Schema Definition language defines built-in primitive data types (i.e., primitive in that these types are not defined in terms of other data types; they exist from the beginning). Totaling eighteen, these primitive data types include `string`, `dateTime`, `Boolean`, `decimal` (the subset of real numbers which can be represented by decimal numerals), and so on. The language defines another twenty-five built-in derived data types (i.e., data types built into the XML Schema Definition Language specification that are defined in terms of primitive and/or other derived data types mentioned elsewhere in the specification). These include `normalizedString` (normalized for whitespace characters), `language` (specialization of `xs:string` encompassing codes for natural languages as defined by an Internet Engineering Task Force guideline), `positiveIntegers`, and so on. The XML Schema Definition language specification also defines mechanisms by which schema designers can derive as many additional data types and content model definitions as they need. As described next, schema designers make extensive use of the ability to derive their own types in all but the very simplest schemas.

Both simple type and complex type definitions can be created using the XML Schema Definition language. The components of a type definition can be embedded (as child elements) within the declaration of an element or attribute, or they can exist separately and be referenced when defining elements and attributes (meaning such a type definition is reusable); the latter approach is considered good practice because it facilitates modularity and the reuse of definitions in multiple element or attribute declarations. A simple type definition references an existing primitive or derived data type to create a new derived data type. Most often new simple types are derived by restricting an existing data type. (Combining simple data types using `<xs:union>` to create a new derived data type is also supported but is less common in library contexts.) Often `<xs:enumeration>` is used in combination with `<xs:restriction>`. For example, issuance is a property in MODS that is used to express how a bibliographic resource was issued. The MODS schema definition document (www.loc.gov/standards/mods/v3/mods-3–5.xsd) derives and names a new simple type called `issuanceDefinition`, and then references this derived type in declaring the `<issuance>` element (see figure 4.3).

The simple type named `issuanceDefinition` defines the allowable values for the `<issuance>` element by restricting the built-in primitive `string` data type to one of the six string values enumerated. A document instance with a content value for the `<issuance>` element that failed to match any of these six enumerated strings would fail validation against the MODS schema.

To declare an element that is allowed (or required) to have additional structure, for example, to have attributes and/or child elements, a complex type definition is needed. The `<typeOfResource>` element is a top-level

```
<xs:simpleType name="issuanceDefinition">
    <xs:restriction base="xs:string">
        <xs:enumeration value="continuing"/>
        <xs:enumeration value="monographic"/>
        <xs:enumeration value="single unit"/>
        <xs:enumeration value="multipart monograph"/>
        <xs:enumeration value="serial"/>
        <xs:enumeration value="integrating resource"/>
    </xs:restriction>
</xs:simpleType>

<xs:element name="issuance" type="issuanceDefinition"/>
```

Figure 4.3 | **Declare the issuance element by referencing the derived issuanceDefinition data type** element in MODS that is used to include a value that expresses the category of the resource being described. The MODS data model enumerates a list of possible values for this property. This value list is translated into a simple type in the MODS XML schema. In addition, <typeOfResource> optionally can have attributes that embellish or refine the meaning of the resource category value selected. A complex type definition is required to declare and define these attributes. Figure 4.4 shows the XML that is used in the MODS XML schema definition document to define the validation rules and constraints for the MODS element <typeOfResource>. Note that certain of these attributes are constrained to a fixed value if present.

```
<xs:simpleType name="resourceTypeDefinition">
      <xs:restriction base="xs:string">
            <xs:enumeration value="text"/>
            <xs:enumeration value="cartographic"/>
            <xs:enumeration value="notated music"/>
            <xs:enumeration value="sound recording-musical"/>
            <xs:enumeration value="sound recording-nonmusical"/>
            <xs:enumeration value="sound recording"/>
            <xs:enumeration value="still image"/>
            <xs:enumeration value="moving image"/>
            <xs:enumeration value="three dimensional object"/>
            <xs:enumeration value="software, multimedia"/>
            <xs:enumeration value="mixed material"/>
            <xs:enumeration value=""/>
      </xs:restriction>
</xs:simpleType>

<xs:complexType name="typeOfResourceDefinition">
      <xs:simpleContent>
            <xs:extension base="resourceTypeDefinition">
                  <xs:attribute name="collection" fixed="yes"/>
                  <xs:attribute name="manuscript" fixed="yes"/>
                  <xs:attribute name="displayLabel" type="xs:string"/>
                  <xs:attribute name="altRepGroup" type="xs:string"/>
                  <xs:attribute name="usage" fixed="primary"/>
            </xs:extension>
      </xs:simpleContent>
</xs:complexType>

<xs:element name="typeOfResource" type="typeOfResourceDefinition"/>
```

Figure 4.4 | **Declaration of the <typeOfResource> element, based on a combination of a complex type definition and a simple type definition**

As illustrated in figure 4.4, `resourceTypeDefinition`, a named simple type definition, is used to enumerate valid content values for the MODS `<typeOfResource>` element. This simple type definition is then referenced in the complex type definition that is used to declare the element's attributes. When declaring the element `<typeOfResource>` it is not necessary to reference the simple type `resourceTypeDefinition` directly, since it is already referenced by the complex type. It is sufficient to reference only the complex type definition when declaring the `<typeOfResource>` element. Note also the use in figure 4.4 of `<xs:extension>` in the complex type definition. The `<xs:extension>` element allows a schema author to augment an existing definition, for example, in this instance to add attribute definitions, when declaring an element. This further illustrates the modularity of XML Schema.

As mentioned, it is not required to name simple and complex type definitions when reuse is unlikely. Instead an anonymous type definition is allowed (leave off the `name` attribute). For example, a simple type definition enumerating valid attribute values can be embedded within a complex type definition or directly within an element or attribute declaration. The complex type definition for the MODS `<namePart>` element illustrates this approach, as shown in figure 4.5. Here the valid values for the "`type`" attribute are provided within an anonymous simple type definition nested within the "`namePartDefinition`" complex type definition.

```
<xs:complexType name="namePartDefinition">
      <xs:simpleContent>
            <xs:extension base="stringPlusLanguage">
                  <xs:attribute name="type">
                        <xs:simpleType>
                              <xs:restriction base="xs:string">
                                    <xs:enumeration value="date"/>
                                    <xs:enumeration value="family"/>
                                    <xs:enumeration value="given"/>
                                    <xs:enumeration value="termsOfAddress"/>
                              </xs:restriction>
                        </xs:simpleType>
                  </xs:attribute>
            </xs:extension>
      </xs:simpleContent>
</xs:complexType>

<xs:element name="namePart" type="namePartDefinition"/>
```

Figure 4.5 | **The declaration for the <namePart> element and its associated complex type definition**

ADDITIONAL MODULARITY FEATURES OF XML SCHEMA

As illustrated in the examples provided above, named simple and complex type definitions and the availability of elements like `<xs:restriction>` and `<xs:extension>` facilitate the creation of schemas and allow a high degree of modularity, facilitating the extension and reuse of preexisting type definitions. The XML Schema Definition language provides additional features to support modularity and extension. Among these are ways to include and import external schemas. The `<xs:include>` element is used when a schema author wants to include definitions and declarations from an external schema with the same target namespace. The `<xs:import>` element is used in order to reference definitions and declarations from a different target namespace. These are powerful tools that make it easy to reference definitions across file boundaries and thereby make it possible to create, develop, and extend complex schemas piecemeal over time.

The concept of grouping is also used in the XML Schema Definition language to facilitate modular authoring and the reuse of generic schema type definitions and declarations. Note in figure 4.5 the reference to the `stringPlusLanguage` definition. This `complexType` definition is shown in figure 4.6 along with the declaration of the `languageAttributeGroup` which is referenced by the `stringPlusLanguage` definition. The `xs:attributeGroup` is a shorthand way to group a set of attributes that will consistently be referenced as a set elsewhere in the schema.

A more nuanced grouping model is that implemented through the `xs:substitutionGroup` attribute. This attribute is used in element declarations, for example, to convey that the element being declared can appear everywhere that another element (declared elsewhere in the schema) is allowed. The MODS schema definition document does not make use of the `xs:substitutionGroup` attribute, but this attribute was used extensively in a set of schemas (http://dublincore.org/schemas/xmls/qdc/2008/02/11/notes/) created to facilitate the use of qualified Dublin Core in the context of the Open Archives Initiative Protocol for Metadata Harvesting. Though now somewhat out of date with regard to advances in recommended options for serializing Dublin Core, these schemas illustrate the modularity of XML schema design in a library application context. See in particular the dcterms.xsd schema in this set. This schema definition declares all the elements (at the time the schemas were last updated) in the Dublin Core Metadata Terms

```
<xs:attributeGroup name="languageAttributeGroup">
      <xs:attribute name="lang" type="xs:string"/>
      <xs:attribute ref="xml:lang"/>
      <xs:attribute name="script" type="xs:string"/>
      <xs:attribute name="transliteration" type="xs:string"/>
</xs:attributeGroup>

<xs:complexType name="stringPlusLanguage">
      <xs:simpleContent>
          <xs:extension base="xs:string">
              <xs:attributeGroup ref="languageAttributeGroup"/>
          </xs:extension>
      </xs:simpleContent>
</xs:complexType>
```

Figure 4.6 | **Declaration of an <attributeGroup> and its use in a complexType definition**

namespace (http://purl.org/dc/terms/). This schema also illustrates the use of the XML Schema Language <import> element.

AN INVALID MODS EXAMPLE

Not all XML applications make use of schemas. Most web browsers, for example, expect only well-formed XML and do not retrieve XML schema definition documents automatically even when referenced in the XML document instances they display. But most XML editing, authoring, and database tools do include validating XML parsers. These applications will report errors and may not process invalid XML once a validation error is encountered even if the XML is well-formed. Figure 4.7 is a MODS XML metadata record describing a digitized book-cover image.

Note that the MODS record shown in figure 4.7 was taken from a set of item-level metadata records for a University of Illinois at Urbana-Champaign online collection of book-cover images and was modified for this illustration. Here the value ("surname") of the type attribute on two instances of the element <namePart> violates the validation constraints shown in figure 4.5. Similarly, the content value ("image") of the <typeOfResource> element violates the constraints declared in the snippet from the MODS schema definition document shown in figure 4.4. Figure 4.8 illustrates the error message returned by the SyncRO Soft oXygen XML editor application (https://www.oxygenxml.com/) for this latter validity violation.

```
<?xml version="1.0" encoding="utf-8"?>
<mods version="3.6"
  xmlns="http://www.loc.gov/mods/v3"
  xmlns:xsi="http://www.w3.org/2001/XMLSchema-instance"
  xsi:schemaLocation="http://www.loc.gov/mods/v3 http://www.loc.gov/
standards/mods/v3/mods-3-6.xsd">
  <identifier type="uri">
http://imagesearchnew.library.illinois.edu/cdm/ref/collection/chicago/id/17
  </identifier>
  <titleInfo><title>50-50: Fighting Chicago's Crime Trusts</title></
titleInfo>
  <name type="personal">
    <namePart type="surname">French</namePart>
    <namePart type="given">George W.</namePart>
    <role> <roleTerm type="text" authority="marcrelator">creator<
/roleTerm></role>
  </name>
  <typeOfResource>image</typeOfResource>
  <accessCondition>Images in this collection were digitized through
the University of Illinois Library's
     participation in the Open Content Alliance and may be used
freely. Attribution to the University of
     Illinois is appreciated. High-resolution images can be downloaded
from the Internet Archive at
     www.archive.org. For further information, email: dcc@library.
uiuc.edu.
  </accessCondition> <physicalDescription><internetMediaType>image/
jp2</internetMediaType></physicalDescription>
  <language><languageTerm>English</languageTerm></language>
  <note>Cover of the book50-50": Fighting Chicago's Crime Trusts.</note>
  <subject><geographic>Chicago (Ill.)</geographic></subject>
  <subject><temporal>1916</temporal></subject>
  <relatedItem type="host" displayLabel="Contained in the Book">
    <titleInfo><title>50-50: fighting Chicago's crime trusts</title>
</titleInfo>
    <name>
      <namePart type="surname">Chamberlin</namePart>
      <namePart type="given">Henry Barrett</namePart>
      <namePart type="date">b. 1867.</namePart>
      <role><roleTerm>author</roleTerm></role>
    </name>
    <location displayLabel="Full text">
<url>http://www.archive.org/stream/5050fightingchic00cham#page/n2/
mode/1up</url>
    </location>
  </relatedItem>
</mods>
```

Figure 4.7 | **An invalid MODS XML record describing a still image resource**

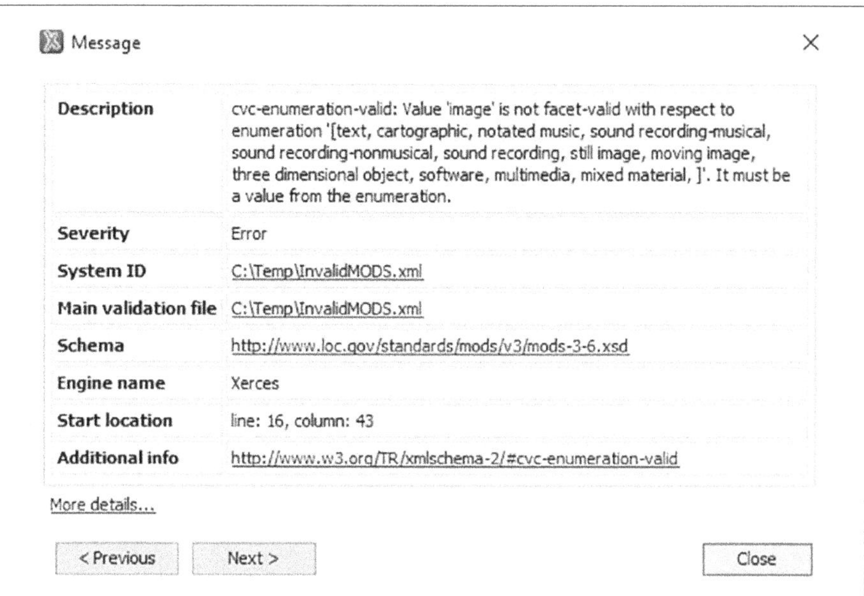

Figure 4.8 | **An XML validation error message as generated by the oXygen XML editor**

Notes

1. The W3C XML Schema Definition Language is defined in three recommendations: David C. Fallside and Patricia Walmsley, eds., *W3C Recommendation: XML Schema Part 0: Primer,* 2nd edition (Cambridge, MA: Massachusetts Institute of Technology, 2004), https://www.w3.org/TR/xmlschema-0/; Shudi Gao, C. M. Sperberg-McQueen, and Henry S. Thompson, eds., *W3C Recommendation: XML Schema Definition Language (XSD) 1.1: Part 1* (Cambridge, MA: Massachusetts Institute of Technology, 2012), https://www.w3.org/TR/xmlschema-1/ ; David Peterson, Shudi Gao, Ashok Malhotra, C. M. Sperberg-McQueen, and Henry S. Thompson, eds., *W3C Recommendation: XML Schema Definition Language (XSD) 1.1: Part 2, Datatypes* (Cambridge, MA: Massachusetts Institute of Technology, 2012), https://www.w3.org/TR/xmlschema-2/. Alternative XML schema languages include RelaxNG (https://www.oasis-open.org/committees/relax-ng/spec.html) and Schematron (http://schematron.com/). RelaxNG, for example, is good for RDF/XML-based implementations.
2. Tim Bray, Dave Hollander, Andrew Layman, and Richard Tobin, eds., *W3C Recommendation: Namespaces in XML 1.1,* 2nd edition (Cambridge, MA: Massachusetts Institute of Technology, 2006), https://www.w3.org/TR/xml-names11/.

AN INTRODUCTION TO XPATH AND XSLT

As described in the preceding chapters, XML provides the means to reveal the intellectual structure of a metadata record. In turn, this access to the structure of a metadata record makes it possible to develop tools that can manipulate, transform, merge, analyze, and otherwise process metadata records on both a small and a large scale. To make such applications efficient and interoperable, ancillary rules (i.e., beyond the foundational syntax and semantics of XML itself) are needed for navigating and acting on metadata serialized as XML. This is where the XML Path Language (XPath), the EXtensible Stylesheet Language for Transformations (XSLT), and the XML Query Language (XQuery) come in. XPath, XSLT, and XQuery are all World Wide Web Consortium (W3C) recommendations.[1]

XPath is an expression-oriented language for navigating the elements, attributes, strings, and other nodes and values found in or derivable from the tree structure of an XML document. XPath is integral to and foundational for both XSLT and XQuery. XSLT is a declarative, rule-based programming language for transforming XML from one schema into another, into HTML, or into plain text files. In XSLT, which has similarities to many functional and stylesheet-based programming languages, templates are created that define actions to take when the XML input matches certain patterns. XQuery (introduced in chapter 8) is a declarative programming language for querying XML documents, both individually and in aggregate. XQuery, which has similarities to relational database query languages, defines directives that are useful for retrieving, interpreting, and processing the metadata contained in XML documents. Both XSLT and XQuery build on and extend the functionality of XPath to accomplish overlapping objectives, albeit in distinctive ways.

XPATH EXPRESSIONS

The primitives or building blocks of XPath are expressions, and the power of XPath stems from path expressions and from the built-in operators, axes, functions, and models used to construct these and other kinds of expressions. (In programming generally, path expressions identify an object by describing how to navigate to it in a tree representation, e.g., in the ordered hierarchy of an XML document; this makes path expressions well-suited for navigating XML metadata.) In XPath, all expressions are composable, meaning that an XPath expression may be composed of more granular XPath expressions, which in turn may be composed of other XPath expressions, and so on. The outcome of evaluating an expression is a sequence of zero or more items, for example, nodes or values. For example, path expressions can be used to identify (from within an XML document tree) a sequence of elements, a sequence of text nodes, an individual attribute node, and so on. Table 5.1 is an incomplete list of the types of expressions currently supported in XPath.

In the XPath data model there are seven kinds of nodes: element, attribute, text, namespace, processing-instruction, comment, and document. The document node is abstract. It represents the parent of the root element of the XML hierarchy and encapsulates the complete XML tree being processed. The nodes of the XML tree being processed are modeled relative to one another along axes; for example, parent axis, child axis, ancestor axis, descendant axis, preceding-sibling axis, following-sibling axis, and so on. Atomic values extracted from the XML tree have a datatype matching one of the primitive datatypes defined in *XML Schema Definition Language Part 2, Datatypes* (e.g., `string`, `boolean`, `decimal`, `date`, etc.) or a datatype derived by restriction from one of these primitive datatypes.[2]

When used within an XSLT or XQuery application, context and scope are key to understanding how an XPath expression is evaluated. For example, when embedded within an XSLT, XPath expressions are evaluated with respect

Table 5.1 | **Categories of XPath expressions (incomplete list)**

CATEGORY OF XPATH EXPRESSION	PURPOSE / EXAMPLES
path expressions	for identifying nodes, values & sequences in an XML tree
primary expressions	string literals such as "hello"; numeric literals such as 7.5
arithmetic expressions	to enable arithmetic operations on atomic values
comparison, conditional and logical expressions	to enable branching and Boolean operations
filter expressions	to filter out subsets of a sequence
"for" expressions	to enable iteration when processing a tree
"let" expressions	to declare a variable and bind it to a value
sequence expressions	for operating over node lists / sequences

to the current context node in the XML tree being transformed as determined by the progress so far of the XSLT as it traverses the tree; that is, based on the outcomes of preceding steps taken to that point in processing XSLT templates. Similarly, XPath variables are scoped according to where in the sequence of XSLT templates or XQuery directives the variable was declared and bound to a value. For example, a variable declared and bound to a value in one XSLT template is not defined or available in any parent or sibling template. Both scope and context have important practical implications when programming with XPath, as will be illustrated later in this and subsequent chapters.

XPath provides a large number of intrinsic operators and functions (discussed below). Most of these operate on nodes, on sequences, and/or on atomic values (e.g., numbers, strings, Boolean values, dates, etc.). Others support aggregation or access to external information. Calls to XPath intrinsic functions can be embedded in XPath expressions. In addition to or instead of taking atomic values as arguments, many XPath functions take a path expression as an argument. XPath also supports references to variables—in XPath variable names are prefixed with a "`$`." In XPath parentheses can be used to enforce the order of precedence during expression evaluation.

In XPath (for the most part), single or double quotes can be used interchangeably when expressing a string literal—for example, the string literals `'hello'` and `"hello"` are equivalent in XPath. This affordance makes it easy to embed string literals inside expressions that appear as the value of an XML attribute; for example, when using XPath within an XSLT stylesheet. In addition, this flexibility is helpful when expressing string literals that include embedded quotes or apostrophes; for example, the string literal `"O'Brien"`.

If necessary to avoid confusion or ambiguity, character entities may be used to represent (aka to escape) quotes or apostrophes that are embedded in string literals—for example, `"O'Brien"`.

XPath supports both unabbreviated and abbreviated path expression syntax. The abbreviated syntax is used for the illustrations that follow. When "`/`" starts a path expression, it represents the document node. Slash characters elsewhere in the path expression denote a single step in the XML tree hierarchy, while the '`@`' symbol is used to prefix attribute names. Double slashes, "`//`", represent all possible intervening steps and can be used at the start of path expressions to match anywhere in an XML tree hierarchy. Expressions used as predicates to filter the result of evaluating an expression appear within square brackets. The details of XPath syntax and semantics are most easily assimilated by examining concrete examples and illustrations. Most of the sample XPath expressions discussed in this chapter (all of which are XPath version 2 or later) are designed to be evaluated against the MARCXML metadata record shown in figure 5.1 (simplified from a real catalog record).

To illustrate how nodes and sequences of nodes from within the MARC XML metadata record in figure 5.1 can be identified for further evaluation or manipulation, figure 5.2 lists a few simple path expressions and the results from evaluating these expressions. As mentioned, an expression appearing in square brackets within another expression acts as a filter for selecting a node(s) from a sequence; for example, a number within square brackets filters by the order of nodes within a sequence returned by the containing expression (thus '`[2]`' selects the second node). If more than one node matches the filter, a subset sequence is returned. Filters can be applied in combination.

XPATH OPERATORS AND FUNCTIONS

Many of XPath's built-in operators and functions are designed to manipulate nodes, sequences, and values identified using path expressions. A handful of these functions are highlighted in figure 5.3. Beyond basic operators involving numeric values (to support addition, subtraction, multiplication, and division), XPath includes additional mathematical operators for finding the modulus (division remainder) of two numeric values, for rounding, and for calculating the floor and ceiling of numeric values. XPath string manipulation functions are especially powerful and cover most use cases that require the parsing of metadata values and strings. Table 5.2 categorizes and lists some of the most frequently used functions (of all kinds) intrinsic to XPath.

```
<?xml version="1.0" encoding="UTF-8"?>
<record>
   <leader>01698cam  22003614a 4500</leader>
   <controlfield tag="001">5439928</controlfield>
   <controlfield tag="005">20080104135038.0</controlfield>
   <controlfield tag="008">070313s2007    ctua     b    001 0 eng  <controlfield>
   <datafield tag="010" ind1=" " ind2=" "><subfield code="a"> 2007009006</
subfield></datafield>
   <datafield tag="020" ind1=" " ind2=" ">
      <subfield code="a">9781591582809 (alk. paper)</subfield>
   </datafield>
  <datafield tag="020" ind1=" " ind2=" ">
       <subfield code="a">1591582806 (alk. paper)</subfield>
   </datafield>
   <datafield tag="029" ind1="1" ind2=" ">
      <subfield code="a">NLGGC</subfield>
      <subfield code="b">302541152</subfield>
   </datafield>
   <datafield tag="035" ind1=" " ind2=" ">
       <subfield code="a">(OCoLC)ocn105428765</subfield>
   </datafield>
   <datafield tag="050" ind1="0" ind2="0">
      <subfield code="a">Z666.7</subfield>
      <subfield code="b">.C65 2007</subfield>
    </datafield>
   <datafield tag="100" ind1="1" ind2=" "><subfield code="a">Cole, Timothy W.
</subfield></datafield>
    <datafield tag="245" ind1="1" ind2="0">
      <subfield code="a">Using the Open Archives Initiative Protocol for
Metadata Harvesting. /</subfield>
      <subfield code="c">Timothy W. Cole and Muriel Foulonneau</subfield>
   </datafield>
   <datafield tag="260" ind1=" " ind2=" ">
      <subfield code="a">Westport, Conn. :</subfield>
      <subfield code="b">Libraries Unlimited,</subfield>
      <subfield code="c">c2007.</subfield>
   </datafield>
   <datafield tag="300" ind1=" " ind2=" ">
      <subfield code="a">xv, 208 p. :</subfield>
      <subfield code="b">ill. ;</subfield>
      <subfield code="c">26 cm.</subfield>
   </datafield>
   <datafield tag="440" ind1=" " ind2="0">
       <subfield code="a">Third millennium cataloging</subfield>
   </datafield>
   <datafield tag="650" ind1=" " ind2="0"><subfield code="a">Metadata
harvesting.</subfield></datafield>
   <datafield tag="610" ind1="2" ind2="0">
      <subfield code="a">Open Archives Initiative.</subfield>
   </datafield>
   <datafield tag="700" ind1="1" ind2=" "><subfield code="a">Foulonneau,
Muriel</subfield></datafield>
</record>
```

Figure 5.1 | **MARC record to use when evaluating sample XPath expressions in this chapter**

PATH EXPRESSION: */record/datafield[1]*
Identifies first datafield (regardless of attribute values) within the root element, record.
Evaluates to a sequence of 1 node:

```
    <datafield tag="010" ind1=" " ind2=" "><subfield code="a">
2007009006</subfield></datafield>
```

PATH EXPRESSION: */record/datafield[@tag="245"][1]/subfield[@code="a"][1]*
Identifies the first subfield with code='a' within the first datafield with tag='245' within record.
Evaluates to a sequence of 1 node:

```
    <subfield code="a">Using the Open Archives Initiative Protocol for
Metadata Harvesting. /</subfield>
```

PATH EXPRESSION: */record/datafield[@tag="020"][2]/subfield[@code="a"][1]*
Identifies the first subfield a within the second datafield 020 within record.
Evaluates to a sequence of 1 node:

```
    <subfield code="a">1591582806 (alk. paper)</subfield>
```

PATH EXPRESSION: *//subfield[3]*
Identifies any and all third subfield elements within any parent anywhere in the metadata record.
Evaluates to a sequence of 2 nodes:

```
    <subfield code="c">c2007.</subfield>
    <subfield code="c">26 cm.</subfield>
```

PATH EXPRESSION: *//datafield[@tag="260"][1]/subfield[3]*
Identifies the third subfield element within the first datafield 260 parent that appears at any level of hierarchy.
Evaluates to a sequence of 1 node:

```
    <subfield code="c">c2007.</subfield>
```

PATH EXPRESSION: */record//subfield[@code='c']*
Identifies all subfield c nodes appearing within any parent within the metadata record.
Evaluates to a sequence of 3 nodes:

```
    <subfield code="c">Timothy W. Cole and Muriel Foulonneau</subfield>
    <subfield code="c">c2007.</subfield>
    <subfield code="c">26 cm.</subfield>
```

Figure 5.2 | **Illustrations of path expressions (evaluated against the XML in figure 5.1)**

EXPRESSION: *string(//datafield[@tag="260"][1])*
This function takes a path expression and returns a string value; note the concatenation of child element values.
Evaluates to a value of datatype string:

" Westport, Conn. : Libraries Unlimited, c2007."

EXPRESSION: *normalize-space(string(//datafield[@tag="260"][1]))*
Evaluates to:

"Westport, Conn. : Libraries Unlimited, c2007."

EXPRESSION: *replace(normalize-space(string(//datafield[@tag="245"][1])), "Open Archives Initiative", "OAI")*
Evaluates to:

"Using the OAI Protocol for Metadata Harvesting. / Timothy W. Cole and Muriel Foulonneau"

EXPRESSION (XPath 3.0): *path(//datafield[@tag="260"][1])*
Evaluates to (note the empty string namespace prefix in this result because no namespace is provided in in figure 5.1 XML):

'/"":*record*[1]/"":*datafield*[9]'

EXPRESSION: *exists(/record/datafield[@tag="856"])*
Evaluates to:

false

EXPRESSION: *count(/record/datafield)*
Evaluates to:

14

EXPRESSION:

concat(substring-after(//datafield[@tag="700"], ","), " ", substring-before(//datafield[@tag="700"], ","))

Evaluates to:

"Muriel Foulonneau"

PATH EXPRESSION: *//subfield[contains(. , 'Muriel')]*
Evaluates to a sequence of 2 nodes:

```
<subfield code="c">Timothy W. Cole and Muriel Foulonneau</subfield>
<subfield code="a">Foulonneau, Muriel</subfield>
```

Figure 5.3 | **Illustrations of XPath expressions that invoke intrinsic XPath functions**

Table 5.2 | **Illustrative subset of XPath functions and operators**

XPATH FUNCTIONS TO	EXAMPLES
Retrieve properties of individual nodes	*local-name(), path(), namespace-uri(), root(), has-children()*
Analyze sequences	*exists(), distinct-values(), empty(), subsequence()*
Calculate aggregate values over sequences	*count(), avg(), sum(), max(), min()*
Manipulate numbers	*round(),abs(),format-number(), format-integer()*
Calculate, parse and format durations	*format-date(), subtract-times(), year-from-dateTime()*
Manipulate strings	*concat(), contains(), normalize-space(), replace(), substring-before(), substring-after(), starts-with(), string()*

Because XPath expressions are composable, these functions can be used in combination, that is, nested. Functions can also be used in path expressions to filter or select nodes, that is, functions can appear in square brackets within path expressions. When using XPath functions the current context node, if needed as an argument for the function, is represented by a dot. (See, for example, the last illustration in figure 5.3—the current context is each node in turn from the node sequence resulting from the evaluation of the `//subfield` path expression.) The XPath operators and functions mentioned here are only the tip of the iceberg. Additional examples are included in subsequent chapters. For full definitions, syntax, and a comprehensive listing of intrinsic XPath operators and functions, see the W3C Recommendation, *XPath and XQuery Functions and Operators 3.1.*[3]

AUTHORING AND DEBUGGING XPATH EXPRESSIONS

XPath expressions are designed to be used within a host; for example, within an XSLT stylesheet or XQuery program, or within an application written in some other programming language. However, it can sometimes be useful for a developer to test and debug XPath expressions in a stand-alone fashion during development. Many XML tools, both desktop and web-based, provide stand-alone environments for authoring and debugging XPath, typically right alongside tools and interfaces provided for authoring and debugging XML, XQuery, XSLT, and so on. At the time this was written, XPath version 2.0 is the most widely supported version, but an increasing number of XML tools are supporting XPath 3.0 as well. XPath 3.1 was ratified by the W3C in March 2017. A few applications allow users to select the version of XPath they want to use.

A common mistake when authoring path expressions is to leave off namespace prefixes. (This can lead to empty result sequences when expressions are evaluated against an XML document instance that uses namespaces.) One of the simplifications in the MARC record shown in figure 5.1 was to leave out the MARCXML namespace declaration. As a result, none of the path expression illustrations in figures 5.2 and 5.3 required any namespace prefixes. When hosted within XSLT, XQuery, or some other application, the namespace bindings of the current context as declared in the host code (e.g., XSLT or XQuery) are inherited by the processor evaluating path expressions. When testing path expressions in stand-alone mode, various approaches may be used to handle namespace references, depending on the XPath processor being used and how it is configured. For example, SyncRO Soft's oXygen XML editor allows users to configure namespace bindings for stand-alone XPath testing through its XPath/XQuery Builder options dialog (under settings). Some tools (including oXygen) can be set to inherit the default namespace and namespace prefixes of the XML root element. Other tools, including some online XPath evaluation tools (e.g., www.freeformatter.com/xpath-tester.html), inherit the namespace prefixes set in the root element, but not that element's default namespace.

Versions 3.0 and 3.1 of the W3C XPath Recommendation introduced BracedURILiterals as a concept important to the processing of XPath expressions. Newer tools, including both oXygen and the FreeFormatter.com online tool, support the use of BracedURILiterals as an alternative way to reference element names that are in a particular namespace; that is, without having to bind a namespace prefix to a URI. If a default namespace declaration attribute had been included in the root record element of the XML shown in figure 5.1, that is:

```
<record xmlns="http://www.loc.gov/MARC21/slim">
```

then a BracedURILiteral could have been used (in lieu of a namespace prefix) to create qualified names for the path expression examples shown in figures 5.2 and 5.3, for example, as illustrated below (equivalent to the first path expression in figure 5.2):

```
/Q{http://www.loc.gov/MARC21/slim}record/Q{http://
www.loc.gov/MARC21/slim}datafield[1]
```

XSLT TEMPLATES AND RESULT-TREES

XSLT is a declarative, rule-based programming language. It is a true stylesheet language in that you can use it to add styling information to XML documents, much as Cascading Style Sheets (CSS) are used to add styling information to HTML pages. But in addition, XSLT can be used for a broad range of nonstyle related tasks, and it is on these tasks we focus here. XSLT can rewrite an XML document valid against one XML schema definition so that it conforms to a wholly different XML schema definition. Alternatively, XSLT can transform or extract information from an XML document to create HTML, XHTML, or plain text. XSLT rewrites and transforms by applying template rules and named templates to a source XML document (the source-tree) in order to generate an output (the result-tree) which can then be saved. Additionally, a single XSLT can generate multiple outputs from a single source-tree, and since version 2, XSLT can process multiple external sources in addition to the source-tree with which it starts.

The power of XSLT stems from its reliance on template rules and pattern matching in combination with its integration of XPath. A template rule associates a pattern with one or more sequence constructors. Patterns in XSLT are implemented using XPath expressions. Sequence constructors create the nodes and values that constitute the output of the template, which can then be added to the result-tree. Semantics for creating sequence constructors allow an XSLT author to write instructions that create nodes and values and define conditional branching and iteration. In this way, the XSLT author controls what is added to the template output. As the XSLT traverses the source-tree, rules, sequence constructors, and other logic within each template are activated when elements of the source-tree match the pattern(s) specified in the template. For maximum flexibility, templates can alternatively be invoked by name. As this was written, version 2 (2007) is the latest XSLT Recommendation that has been ratified by the W3C. XSLT Version 3.0 reached Candidate Recommendation status in February 2017.[4] The expectation is that XSLT version 3.0 will fully align with XPath versions 3.0 and 3.1. Pending ratification, developers must be cognizant of differences in the versions of XPath and XSLT supported by different tools and XSLT processors.

Figure 5.4 shows a simple template rule and its output when evaluated against the metadata record shown in figure 5.1. The instructions of this template (`xsl:` is the namespace prefix for the instructions, i.e., the XSLT elements, in this and following examples) are implemented for each node in the source-tree that matches the template's path expression, i.e., the value of the template's

```
<xsl:template match='//datafield[@tag="100" or @tag="700"]'>
    <creator>
        <xsl:value-of select="."/>
    </creator>
</xsl:template>
```

Output of this template (line breaks added for readability):

```
<creator>Cole, Timothy W.</creator>
<creator>Foulonneau, Muriel</creator>
```

Figure 5.4 | **A simple template rule (i.e., no name attribute)**

match attribute. Thus the template is evaluated once for each matching node in the XML source-tree. For each evaluation, the current context is the matching node from the source-tree.

This example illustrates two frequently used features of XSLT. First, note that the `<creator>` element, because it is not in the XSLT namespace and so is not interpreted by the XSLT processor as a template rule, declaration, or instruction to be processed, constitutes a literal result element; that is, the open and close `<creator>` tags are simply added to the template output as is. This is one way to add an element (with or without attributes) directly to a template's output and to the result-tree. Second, note the use of the element `<xsl:value-of>`. If this element is empty (as in this instance), then the `select` attribute must be specified. When used this way, the XSLT processor sees this element as a placeholder that should be replaced in the template output with the value resulting from the evaluation of the XPath expression contained in the `select` attribute. Specifying a path expression that resolves to a node-list does not raise an error; rather, the values of all of the nodes in the node-list are concatenated, and the result is added to the output.

Figure 5.5 illustrates how to achieve the same output using a named template. This template would be invoked (called) explicitly by name from elsewhere within the stylesheet, for example:

```
<xsl:call-template name="authorTemplate"/>
```

Invoking a template by name does not change context. Accordingly, the `<xsl:for-each>` element is required in this template to select and iterate through matching nodes and to ensure that the elements inside of the template are evaluated only for the nodes within the metadata record that match the path expression given by the select attribute of the `<xsl:for-each>` element.

```
<xsl:template name='authorTemplate'>
      <xsl:for-each select='//datafield[@tag="100" or @tag="700"]'>
          <creator>
               <xsl:value-of select="."/>
          </creator>
      </xsl:for-each>
  </xsl:template>
```

Output of this template (line breaks added for readability):

```
<creator>Cole, Timothy W.</creator>
<creator>Foulonneau, Muriel</creator>
```

Figure 5.5 | **A simple *named* template (i.e., no match attribute)**

```
<xsl:template match='//datafield[@tag = "100" or @tag = "700"]'>
      <xsl:element name="h3" namespace="http://www.w3.org/1999/xhtml">
          <xsl:attribute name="style">font-style:italic; color:red
</xsl:attribute>
          <xsl:value-of select="."/>
      </xsl:element>
  </xsl:template>
```

Output of this template:

```
   <h3 xmlns="http://www.w3.org/1999/xhtml" style="font-style:italic;
color:red">Cole, Timothy W.</h3>

   <h3 xmlns="http://www.w3.org/1999/xhtml" style="font-style:italic;
color:red">Foulonneau, Muriel</h3>
```

Figure 5.6 | **A template rule (i.e., no name attribute) that creates a snippet of HTML**

Note that each time the `<xsl:for-each> select` attribute is matched, the context does change to the matching node. The element `<xsl:for-each>` is therefore said to change the focus of the XSLT processor; that is, it changes which node in the XML source-tree is the current context.

Figure 5.6 is again a template rule, but here a snippet of HTML is being created. The element, `<h3>`, is added to the result-tree using the `<xsl:element>` instruction. This example also illustrates how attributes and attribute values can be added to a template's output using `<xsl:attribute>` and how the elements included in the output can be associated with namespaces.

In XSLT, note that templates can have both a name attribute and a match attribute—that is, a template can be both a template rule and a named template.

If such a hybrid template is invoked as a rule through its match attribute, then the context is changed accordingly. If the hybrid template is invoked by name, then the context does not change. In most metadata use cases, developers do not create templates that are simultaneously a template rule and a named template. This avoids confusion.

THE STRUCTURE OF AN XSLT STYLESHEET

The core syntax of XSLT is XML. XSLT stylesheets are well formed and valid XML document instances. XSLT stylesheets have a root element, `<xsl:stylesheet>`, and it is in the `www.w3.org/1999/XSL/Transform` namespace, which is typically bound to the namespace prefix "`xsl:`". (For historical reasons, the element `<xsl:transform>` is allowed as a synonym to `<xsl:stylesheet>`. Version 3.0 also introduces an additional root element option, `<xsl:package>`, which along with the already existing elements `<xsl:import>` and `<xsl:include>` facilitates modularity and the use of XSLT template libraries.) XSLT also relies heavily on XML namespaces. The semantics of XSLT (simple and complex type definitions and element and attribute names) are all in a single namespace. Any additional namespace prefix bindings that may be required for evaluating path expressions and for associating namespaces with literal result elements added to the result-tree can be declared in the host XSLT by adding attributes to the root `<xsl:stylesheet>` element. To facilitate the use of XML namespaces, XSLT introduces an added namespace declaration attribute, `xsl:xpath-default-namespace`, which can be used to declare a default namespace binding for evaluating XPath expressions contained within the stylesheet.

While XSLT is considered a rule-based (rather than a declarative) programming language, and while XSLT templates are thought of as rules, the W3C XSLT Recommendation categorizes most XSLT elements as either instructions or declarations. (The elements `<xsl:variable>` and `<xsl:param>` are typically counted as both.) Instruction elements are used in sequence constructors to build template outputs and the result-tree. By definition, an XSLT sequence constructor is comprised of XSLT instructions, literal result elements, and/or text nodes. Declarative elements, by contrast, typically appear as direct children of the root element of an XSLT (e.g., `<xsl:stylesheet>`), not in templates. Declarative elements define output settings, declare and bind global variables, declare and set default values for stylesheet parameters, facilitate the reuse of external template libraries, and set options such as what to do with whitespace

Table 5.3 | **Incomplete list of instructional and declarative XSLT elements**

CATEGORY / ROLE OF XSLT ELEMENT	EXAMPLES
root elements	*xsl:stylesheet, xsl:transform, xsl:package*
Instructional elements (these elements appear in templates) to:	
generate nodes or values	*xsl:element, xsl:attribute, xsl:value-of, xsl:text*
iterate or branch conditionally	*xsl:for-each, xsl:if, xsl:choose, xsl:when, xsl:otherwise*
invoke templates	*xsl:apply-templates, xsl:call-template*
perform specialized tasks	*xsl:analyze-string* (regex), *xsl:sort, xsl:for-each-group*
Declarative elements (elements are typically direct children of xsl:stylesheet) to:	
bind variables and parameters	*xsl:variable, xsl:param* (instructional when in templates)
define what will be done with whitespace	*xsl:preserve-space, xsl:strip-space*
integrate / reuse external XSLT templates	*xsl:package, xsl:include, xsl:import*
define output method and settings	*xsl:output*

found in the source-tree. (This last function can be important when processing MARC records, since the whitespace in MARC leader and control fields is meaningful.) Table 5.3 lists a few of the most frequently used XSLT elements and organizes them by category, that is, instruction or declaration.

An XSLT stylesheet may contain any number of template rules and named templates, but most XSLT stylesheets will have a top-level template rule that matches the document node; this template manages the overall transformation flow. Through the use of the `<xsl:apply-templates>` instruction element (for invoking template rules) and the `<xsl:call-template>` instruction element (for invoking named templates), this top-level template controls which nodes of the source-tree are evaluated against the other templates of the stylesheet and in what order this is done. Though not required, most XSLT stylesheets also include an `<xsl:output>` element. This element defines the format of the anticipated output, including whether the output is XML, HTML, XHTML, plain text, or some other tool-specific format (rarely used). If absent, the XSLT processor assumes that an `<xsl:output>` element with no attributes is present.

Figure 5.7 is a complete XSLT stylesheet. The root node, `<xsl:stylesheet>`, includes a namespace declaration (binding the prefix `xsl:` to the XSLT namespace) and a version attribute informing the XSLT processor

```
<?xml version="1.0" encoding="UTF-8"?>
<xsl:stylesheet xmlns:xsl="http://www.w3.org/1999/XSL/Transform" version="2.0">
     <xsl:output method="xhtml" omit-xml-declaration="yes" include-content
-type="no"/>
    <xsl:template match="/">
      <xsl:element name="html" namespace="http://www.w3.org/1999/xhtml">
        <xsl:element name="head" namespace="http://www.w3.org/1999/xhtml">
          <xsl:element name="title" namespace="http://www.w3.org/1999/xhtml">
              Authors
          </xsl:element>
         </xsl:element>
         <xsl:element name="body" namespace="http://www.w3.org/1999/xhtml">
           <xsl:apply-templates select='//datafield[@tag="100" or @tag="700"]'/>
         </xsl:element>
        </xsl:element>
    </xsl:template>
    <xsl:template match='//datafield[@tag = "100" or @tag = "700"]'>
      <xsl:element name="h3" namespace="http://www.w3.org/1999/xhtml">
       <xsl:attribute name="style">font-style:italic; color:red
       </xsl:attribute>
            <xsl:value-of select="."/>
        </xsl:element>
    </xsl:template>
</xsl:stylesheet>
```

Result-tree of this stylesheet (assuming the XML of figure 5.1 as source-tree):

```
<html xmlns="http://www.w3.org/1999/xhtml">
   <head>
     <title> Authors</title>
   </head>
   <body>
      <h3 style="font-style:italic; color:red">Cole, Timothy W.</h3>
      <h3 style="font-style:italic; color:red">Foulonneau, Muriel</h3>
   </body>
</html>
```

igure 5.7 | **A simple, complete XSLT stylesheet with sample output**

ıat this stylesheet was written to conform to XSLT version 2.0. This stylesheet includes wo template rules, the first matching on the document node, and the second matching n occurrences in the source-tree of datafield elements having tag attribute values of ither `100` or `700`. An `<xsl:output>` declaration element is provided as a sibling in ıe stylesheet tree of the two template rules. This element informs the XSLT processor :hrough the method attribute) that the result-tree of this stylesheet will be an XHTML document. Other attributes of the `<xsl:output>`, element tell the XSLT processor not to include an HTML meta tag specifying `Content-Type` in the output, and not to include the XML declaration at the top of the result-tree.

The stylesheet shown in figure 5.7 illustrates how to invoke rule templates using `<xsl:apply-templates>`. This instructional element has an optional attribute, `select`. Though not required, this attribute is frequently used to provide a path expression identifying the nodes in the source-tree that need to be checked at this stage of the transform against the available rule templates of the stylesheet. Otherwise, by default the entire context (in this instance the document node, i.e., the complete source-tree) is checked against all rule-templates in the XSLT stylesheet. Specifying which nodes of the source-tree are to be checked against the stylesheet's rule templates allows the XSLT author to order the result-tree. (By default, template rule matches are applied in the order in which the match is encountered in the source-tree.) Also, because XSLT includes a number of default, built-in template rules, if `<xsl:apply-templates>` is used without specifying a path expression in a `select` attribute, then any nodes of the source-tree that do not match an explicit template rule in the stylesheet will be evaluated against XSLT's implicit, built-in templates for matches. Because there is a built-in template that indiscriminately matches text nodes, typically the result of not including a select attribute on `<xsl:apply-templates>` is that the values of any unmatched text nodes get added directly to the template output and the result-tree. If the source-tree contains an unanticipated pattern, unanticipated content may appear in the result-tree because of this behavior. (So always use the `<xsl:apply-templates>` `select` attribute.)

VARIABLES AND PARAMETERS IN XSLT

The `<xsl:variable>` element is used to declare a variable and bind a value to it. XSLT variables allow stylesheet authors to declare and bind a variable at a point in the transform flow of their choosing and then reference this variable at subsequent points in the transform flow. If the `<xsl:variable>` element contains a value or node, then that value or node is bound to the variable's name (identifier) as given by the `<xsl:variable>` `name` attribute. If the variable contains a sequence constructor, the result of evaluating the sequence constructor is bound to the variable name. If the `<xsl:variable>` element is empty, then the `select` attribute is required and the result of evaluating the expression contained in the `select` attribute is bound to the variable name.

XSLT parameters are created in a similar fashion using the `<xsl:param>` element, with the added feature that any default value binding set when declaring a parameter may be overridden when the stylesheet or template referencing the parameter is invoked. XSLT variables are a convenience for stylesheet authors—for example, they obviate the need to reenter complicated sequence constructors or XPath expressions every time they are used. Parameters can be essential when invoking general-purpose, reusable stylesheets, templates, or functions, and when using recursion (discussed below).

However, to programmers who are well-versed in imperative, procedural programming languages, XSLT variables and parameters will seem more like scoped constants than variables. Depending on where they are inserted, the `<xsl:variable>` and `<xsl:param>` elements bind a name to a value globally for an entire stylesheet (when the element appears as the immediate child of xsl:stylesheet) or locally within the scope of the particular template or sequence constructor in which the element appears. Once this binding happens, there is no statement in XSLT for altering the value of a variable or parameter; that is, there is no *assignment operator* as is common in many programming languages. Globally scoped variables and parameters can be referenced from anywhere in a stylesheet. The value of a globally declared variable or parameter is determined at the start of a transform (or for a parameter, it is set when the stylesheet is invoked) and cannot be changed once set. If an `<xsl:variable>` or an `<xsl:parameter>` element appears within a sequence constructor or template, the variable or parameter has local scope. The variable or parameter can only be referenced within that sequence constructor or template. The value is reset each time the template or sequence constructor is invoked.

Figure 5.8 shows an augmented version of the stylesheet introduced in figure 5.7. Two named templates, `titleHead` and `titleH2`, have been added, as well as two `<xsl:call-template>` elements and a globally scoped variable (`$title`). The `<xsl:variable>` element declaring `$title` includes a `select` attribute containing the path expression for subfield '`$a`' of the MARC 245 field (Title Statement). The resolution of this path expression provides the value that is bound to the variable `$title`. The `<xsl:call-template>` instructions and corresponding named templates are used to insert this value into the HTML title element (within the HTML head element) and later into an `<h2>` element in the body of the HTML page. The complete result-tree is shown at the bottom of figure 5.8. This is a simple illustration of the use of an XSLT variable, but the reader can easily anticipate more sophisticated scenarios involving variables and parameters.

```
<?xml version="1.0" encoding="UTF-8"?>
<xsl:stylesheet xmlns:xsl="http://www.w3.org/1999/XSL/Transform"
version="2.0">
    <xsl:output method="xhtml" omit-xml-declaration="yes" include-content-
type="no"/>
    <xsl:variable name="title" select='//datafield[@tag="245"]/subfield[@
code="a"]'/>

    <xsl:template match="/">
      <xsl:element name="html" namespace="http://www.w3.org/1999/xhtml">
        <xsl:element name="head" namespace="http://www.w3.org/1999/xhtml">
           <xsl:call-template name="titleHead"/>
        </xsl:element>
        <xsl:element name="body" namespace="http://www.w3.org/1999/xhtml">
            <xsl:call-template name="titleH2"/>
            <xsl:apply-templates select='//datafield[@tag="100" or @
tag="700"]'/>
        </xsl:element>
      </xsl:element>
    </xsl:template>

    <xsl:template name="titleHead">
       <xsl:element name="title" namespace="http://www.w3.org/1999/xhtml">
          <xsl:value-of select="$title"/>
       </xsl:element>
    </xsl:template>

    <xsl:template name="titleH2">
       <xsl:element name="h2" namespace="http://www.w3.org/1999/xhtml">
          <xsl:value-of select="$title"/>
       </xsl:element>
    </xsl:template>

    <xsl:template match='//datafield[@tag = "100" or @tag = "700"]'>
       <xsl:element name="h3" namespace="http://www.w3.org/1999/xhtml">
          <xsl:attribute name="style">font-style:italic; color:red
          </xsl:attribute>
          <xsl:value-of select="."/>
       </xsl:element>
    </xsl:template>
</xsl:stylesheet>
```

Result-tree of this stylesheet (assuming the XML of figure 5.1 as source-tree):

```
<html xmlns="http://www.w3.org/1999/xhtml">
   <head>
      <title>Using the Open Archives Initiative Protocol for Metadata
```

```
Harvesting. /</title>
   </head>
   <body>
      <h2>Using the Open Archives Initiative Protocol for Metadata
Harvesting. /</h2>
      <h3 style="font-style:italic; color:red">Cole, Timothy W.</h3>
      <h3 style="font-style:italic; color:red">Foulonneau, Muriel</h3>
   </body>
</html>
```

Figure 5.8 | **An XSLT stylesheet illustrating the use of a global variable**

RECURSION IN XSLT

Recursion can be a useful approach in XSLT to address certain metadata workflows. In XSLT, recursion is most often implemented by constructing a template that invokes itself as many times as necessary in order to accomplish a specific task. An illustrative recursion use case is the parsing of subject headings that may contain varying numbers of subdivisions. A template is created to extract and remove the first component from the heading. After this is done, the template calls itself to process the rest of the string with this first component removed. This is done recursively until the heading has been fully parsed. For example, figure 5.9 shows a fragment of an XHTML bibliographic record display as generated by a web-friendly library online public-access catalog. Three subject headings assigned to a book are shown (the rest of the record has been deleted for clarity). A librarian reading this display would recognize from the punctuation (i.e., the "—") that each subject heading is composed of a name or main term concatenated with one or two subdivision headings. To differentiate these as separate elements in the XSLT result-tree markup, it is necessary to parse the value of each of the relevant table cells (`<td>` elements) and separate out subject heading components based on the '—' characters.

A stylesheet to do this using recursion is shown in figure 5.10. The document-node matching template (`match="/"`) creates a root element (`<subjects>`) for the result-tree and then adds a child element (`<heading>`) for each source-tree table cell (`<td>`) containing a subject heading. For each `<td>` it then calls a named template (`parseSubject`), binding the template's parameter `$ctext` to the string value of the `<td>` cell and `$level` to the string '`mainTermOrName`.' Each time invoked, the template branches on the presence or absence of '–' in `$ctext`. If present, it first creates a new node in the result-tree. The name given to this new output element is the value `$level`

```
<html>
    <head>
        <title>subjects</title>
    </head>
    <body>
       <table>
           <tr>
             <td align="right" valign="top">Subject (LCSH):</td>
             <td>Lincoln, Abraham, 1809-1865 -- Military leadership.</td>
           </tr>
           <tr>
             <td/>
             <td>United States -- History -- Civil War, 1861-1865.</td>
           </tr>
           <tr>
             <td/>
             <td>United States -- Politics and government -- 1861-1865.</td>
           </tr>
       </table>
    </body>
</html>
```

Figure 5.9 | **Fragment of an HTML (version 4) table extracted from a bibliographic catalog record**

('mainTermOrName' the first time through). The content of this new output element is the string-before '–'. The template then calls itself, passing as new value for `$ctext` the string-after '–' and as new value for `$level` the string '`subdivision`.' This recurs until `$ctext` no longer contains '–', at which point the remaining `$ctext` is added to the result-tree in a final instance of the element `<subdivision>`. The result-tree created assuming as source-tree the HTML from figure 5.9 is shown at the bottom of figure 5.10.

This example using named templates illustrates a relatively straightforward use of recursion, but is not compelling. Since the introduction in XPath version 2 of support for regular expressions, another approach for this use case is to use the XPath `tokenize` function; for example, for the second cell of the third table row from the original HTML shown in figure 5.9:

```
tokenize(/html/body/table/tr[3]/td[2], '—')
```

The first argument in this function call is an XPath expression identifying the node in the source tree on which to operate. The second argument is the pattern to match which is assumed to be a regular expression (in this instance the string '—' suffices). The function in this instance then would return a

```
<?xml version="1.0" encoding="UTF-8"?>
<xsl:stylesheet xmlns:xsl="http://www.w3.org/1999/XSL/Transform"
version="2.0">
   <xsl:output method="xml" omit-xml-declaration="yes" indent="yes"/>
   <xsl:template match="/">
     <xsl:element name="subjects">
       <xsl:for-each select="/html/body/table/tr/td[2]">
          <xsl:element name="heading">
             <xsl:call-template name="parseSubject">
                <xsl:with-param name="ctext">
                   <xsl:value-of select="."/>
                </xsl:with-param>
                <xsl:with-param name="level" select="'mainTermOrName'">
                </xsl:with-param>
             </xsl:call-template>
          </xsl:element>
         </xsl:for-each>
       </xsl:element>
   </xsl:template>
   <xsl:template name="parseSubject">
       <xsl:param name="ctext"/>
       <xsl:param name="level"/>
       <xsl:choose>
           <xsl:when test="contains($ctext, ' --')">
               <xsl:element name="{$level}">
                  <xsl:value-of select="substring-before($ctext, ' --')"/>
               </xsl:element>
               <xsl:call-template name="parseSubject">
                  <xsl:with-param name="ctext" select="substring-after
($ctext, ' --')"/>
                  <xsl:with-param name="level" select="'subdivision'"/>
               </xsl:call-template>
           </xsl:when>
           <xsl:otherwise>
               <xsl:element name="{$level}">
                  <xsl:value-of select="$ctext"/>
               </xsl:element>
           </xsl:otherwise>
       </xsl:choose>
   </xsl:template>
</xsl:stylesheet>
```

Result-tree of this stylesheet (assuming figure 5.9 as source-tree):

```
<subjects>
  <heading>
     <mainTermOrName>Lincoln, Abraham, 1809-1865</mainTermOrName>
     <subdivision>Military leadership.</subdivision>
  </heading>
  <heading>
     <mainTermOrName>United States</mainTermOrName>
     <subdivision>History</subdivision>
     <subdivision>Civil War, 1861-1865.</subdivision>
  </heading>
  <heading>
     <mainTermOrName>United States</mainTermOrName>
     <subdivision>Politics and government</subdivision>
     <subdivision>1861-1865.</subdivision>
  </heading>
</subjects>
```

igure 5.10 | **A stylesheet using recursion to parse string values extracted from a source-tree**

sequence of three text values, that is, "`United States`," "`Politics and government`," and "`1861-1865`," which can then be used to build the desired node(s) in the result-tree.

A more compelling illustration of recursion, one using template rules instead of named templates, is the identity transform. An identity transform in XSLT duplicates the source-tree in the result-tree. As illustrated in figure 5.11, with minor modification the identity transform can be the basis for creating an easy and efficient stylesheet when all that is needed is a minor modification to an otherwise arbitrary source-tree (e.g., to add a simple attribute to an element when present). The stylesheet in figure 5.11 contains two template rules. The first matches all nodes and attributes of the current context other than the one matched by the second template (which being more specific takes priority during processing). The first template copies its context node to the result-tree and then applies templates for all child nodes and attributes (the asterisk is a wild card), in essence calling itself recursively for all attributes and child nodes—except a child node that matches the second template. The second template, which matches on the first cell (`td[1]`) of the first row (`tr[1]`) of the table, modifies that data cell (`<td>`) by adding a `style` attribute. It then (as with the first template) applies templates for all attributes and child nodes. Note the use of '`node()`' rather than '`/*`' in the `match` path expression. This ensures that all kinds of nodes recognized by XPath are processed, rather than just element nodes. Note also that attributes must be explicitly matched, since attributes are not nodes on an element's child axis. Leaving the `@*` out would mean that source-tree attributes would not be replicated in the result-tree.

TESTING AND DEBUGGING XSLT STYLESHEETS

Obviously, to test and debug an XSLT stylesheet you need both the stylesheet and at least one appropriate XML metadata record to serve as the source-tree for the transform. You then need a tool or web application that will attempt to perform the transform and report any errors. The transform if successful will result in a third resource, the result-tree, which needs to either be saved (for later inspection) or immediately viewed. Given the vagaries of library metadata, keep in mind that just because an XSLT successfully transforms one of your XML metadata records does not mean it will successfully transform all of your XML metadata records. An XSLT should be tested over a representative sample of the metadata records on which you wish to use it.

```
<?xml version="1.0" encoding="UTF-8"?>
<xsl:stylesheet xmlns:xsl="http://www.w3.org/1999/XSL/Transform"
version="2.0">
    <xsl:output method="xhtml" omit-xml-declaration="yes" indent="yes"/>

    <xsl:template match="@* | node()">
        <xsl:copy>
            <xsl:apply-templates select="@* | node()"/>
        </xsl:copy>
    </xsl:template>

    <xsl:template match="/html/body/table/tr[1]/td[1]">
        <xsl:element name="td">
            <xsl:attribute name="style">color: red</xsl:attribute>
            <xsl:apply-templates select="@* | node()"/>
        </xsl:element>
    </xsl:template>

</xsl:stylesheet>
```

Result-tree of this stylesheet (assuming figure 5.9 as source-tree):

```
<html>
    <head>
      <title>subjects</title>
    </head>
    <body>
       <table>
         <tr>
           <td style="color: red" align="right" valign="top">Subject
           (LCSH):</td>
           <td>Lincoln, Abraham, 1809-1865 -- Military leadership.
           </td>
         </tr>
         <tr>
           <td/>
           <td>United States -- History -- Civil War, 1861-1865.</td>
         </tr>
         <tr>
           <td/>
          <td>United States -- Politics and government -- 1861-1865.</td>
         </tr>
       </table>
    </body>
</html>
```

Figure 5.11 | **A modified identity transform that adds a style attribute to one data cell in a table**

The sophistication of the XSLT debugging tool you choose will depend on the complexity of your transform, the format (XML or HTML) of your result-tree, and the scale of your project; for example, the number of metadata records you need to process. For small projects involving relatively straightforward and simple XSLT (like the illustrations in this chapter), a web-based XML transform service may be sufficient (e.g., www.freeformatter.com/xsl-transformer.html). As this was being written, it is also still possible to use a web browser to debug simple XSLT instances. Most current web browsers have their own embedded XSLT processors that support at least XSLT version 1.0. In theory this can be a good way for developers to test simple, stand-alone XSLT stylesheets designed to generate HTML result-trees that might best be viewed using a web browser. However, note that most web browsers do not yet (as of when this was written) fully support XSLT 2.0 (let alone XSLT 3.0). Additionally, increasing sensitivity to workstation and web server security can create some obstacles to using web browsers to debug XSLTs.

To transform an XML document instance in a web browser, the following processing instruction should be added to the XML file immediately below the XML declaration (i.e., in the prolog):

```
<?xml-stylesheet type='text/xsl' href=' . . . ' ?>
```

where '. . .' is replaced by the URL from which the XSLT stylesheet can be obtained. This can be a relative URL address (which is useful when both XML and XSLT are co-located in the same folder). Note that for historical reasons, the media (MIME) type specified in this processing instruction is `text/xsl` rather than the currently registered media type for XSLT, `application/xslt+xml`. Security settings can prevent a web browser from carrying out the transform if

- the XML (source-tree) and XSLT are on different servers (cross-origin error);
- the XSLT is not delivered with a valid media (MIME) type (should be either `text/xsl` or `application/xslt+xml`);
- the XML and XSLT are on the local file system (some web browsers treat this situation as if the XML and XSLT came from separate servers, giving an error message such as: "file: URLs are treated as unique security origins").

At the very least, anticipate security warning messages if you attempt to debug locally stored XSLTs in your web browser. For more about associating style sheets (both XSLT and CSS) with XML metadata records, see the W3C Recommendation on the subject.[5]

For larger projects and more complex XSLT development, a proper XSLT development tool is required. Most major desktop XML editors include or make available as add-ons sophisticated and powerful tools for creating and debugging XSLT. Examples that are widely used in the library community include SyncRO Soft's oXygen XML editor (https://www.oxygenxml.com/), Altova's XMLSpy XML editor (https://www.altova.com/xmlspy.html), and the XSL/XSLT Tools from Stylus Studio (www.stylusstudio.com/xslt.html). These tools are in essence integrated development environments (IDEs) for the creation and development of XSLT stylesheets. Like IDEs for major programming languages, these tools allow a developer to step through the transform line-by-line to check variable and parameter values, see where in the source-tree a particular path expression points, see how conditional expressions resolve, and so on. Most also provide explanatory tips, real-time syntax checking, and prompts to help with developing XSLTs.

CONCLUSION

As libraries collect and license an increasing number of born digital and retrospectively digitized resources, metadata librarians and catalogers need to manage and manipulate an increasing number of bibliographic descriptions in digital form. Often these descriptive records are shared and/or stored in XML. In order to accomplish their assignments in a timely matter, metadata librarians and catalogers must develop sustainable and scalable workflows. XPath and XSLT are powerful standards that can be implemented in many cataloging and metadata workflows to make the editing, updating, reusing, sharing, and maintenance of XML metadata records easier and quicker. XPath and XSLT require a significant investment of time to learn, but in the long run, the efficiencies possible with these technologies can be well worth it.

Notes

1. Jonathan Robie, Michael Dyck and Josh Spiegel, eds., *W3C Recommendation: XML Path Language (XPath) 3.1* (Cambridge, MA: Massachusetts Institute of Technology, 2017), https://www.w3.org/TR/xpath-31/; Michael Kay, ed., *W3C Recommendation: XSL Transformations (XSLT) Version 2.0* (Cambridge, MA: Massachusetts Institute of Technology, 2007), https://www.w3.org/TR/xslt20/; Jonathan Robie, Michael Dyck, and Josh Spiegel, eds., *W3C Recommendation: XQuery 3.1: An XML Query Language* (Cambridge, MA: Massachusetts Institute of Technology, 2017), https://www.w3.org/TR/xquery-31/.

2. David Peterson, Shudi Gao, Ashok Malhotra, C. M. Sperberg-McQueen, and Henry S. Thompson, eds., *W3C Recommendation: XML Schema Definition Language (XSD) 1.1: Part 2 , Datatypes* (Cambridge, MA: Massachusetts Institute of Technology, 2012), https://www.w3.org/TR/xmlschema11–2/.
3. Michael Kay, ed., *W3C Recommendation: XPath and XQuery Functions and Operators 3.1* (Cambridge, MA: Massachusetts Institute of Technology, 2017), https://www.w3.org/TR/xpath-functions-31/.
4. Michael Kay, ed., *W3C Candidate Recommendation: XSL Transformations (XSLT) Version 3.0* (Cambridge, MA: Massachusetts Institute of Technology, 2017), https://www.w3.org/TR/xslt-30/.
5. James Clark, Simon Pieters, and Henry S. Thompson, *W3C Recommendation: Associating Style Sheets with XML Documents 1.0 (Second Edition)* (Cambridge, MA: Massachusetts Institute of Technology, 2010), https://www.w3.org/TR/xml-stylesheet/.

CATALOGING WORKFLOWS USING XSLT

Use of the EXtensible Stylesheet Language for Transformations (XSLT) has significantly improved library cataloging workflows over the last decade, and XSLT offers the potential for additional improvements in workflow efficiencies in coming years. XSLT is especially useful when transforming metadata from one metadata schema to another or when adding new information into metadata records during batch processing. This chapter will describe and explore two XSLT-based cataloging workflows, one simple and the other complex. Both of these workflows are currently in use at the University of Illinois at Urbana-Champaign. The first illustrates how easily and simply XSLT can be used for basic metadata enhancement work. The second, more complex illustration shows how XSLT can be used to transform metadata records from one standard to another.

WORKFLOW 1

ADDING HATHITRUST DIGITAL LIBRARY HANDLES INTO PRINTED BOOKS' METADATA

Background: Established in 2008, the HathiTrust Digital Library (https://www.hathitrust.org/) serves as an access and preservation repository for library resources digitized from the print collections of its member institutions, which number more than 120 academic, special, and public libraries located around the world. From its publicly accessible website, HathiTrust provides integrated search and discovery across all deposited digital resources, making available for viewing by the public complete scans of digitized resources where allowed by copyright. The University of Illinois at Urbana-Champaign Library (henceforth the Illinois Library) has been contributing digitized contents to HathiTrust since 2011 and uses HathiTrust as a key discovery and preservation repository for digitized books. The Illinois Library also decided to add HathiTrust-produced handles, that is, persistent, http-scheme Uniform Resource Identifiers (URIs), into local catalog records in order to provide direct access from the university's online public access catalog (OPAC) system. (When de-referenced, i.e., when entered into the location bar of a web browser, HathiTrust handles take a user to the digitized resource.) A cataloging workflow was created to add HathiTrust handles to local catalog metadata describing the items that we have digitized and contributed to HathiTrust.

HathiTrust naming and identifier conventions: To trigger the ingestion of items into the HathiTrust Digital Library, each contributing institution submits item-level bibliographic metadata serialized as MARCXML. At the Illinois Library we begin by extracting a MARCXML record from the catalog for each item to be submitted to the HathiTrust. Additional HathiTrust-requested information is then added to these records using the MARC datafield 955, in accordance with the dictates of a web page (https://www.hathitrust.org/bib_data_submission) maintained by HathiTrust. The contents of the subfields we include for HathiTrust in datafield 955 are detailed in table 6.1.

Datafield 955 subfield `$b` is the only one that is always required because the value of this subfield is a unique item identifier (at least locally) and is incorporated (along with an institution-specific 'namespace' prefix) into the

Table 6.1 | **HathiTrust bibliographic metadata specification includes item-specific information**

MARC FIELD	HOW TO USE	REQUIRED/OPTIONAL
955 $b	Local item identifier (e.g., barcode) or ARK identifier (Internet Archive[4] content)	Required
955 $q	Internet Archive identifier (if the item is in the Internet Archive)	Required IF the item is in the Internet Archive
955 $v	Enumeration and chronology	Optional

HathiTrust handle that is created for the item. The Illinois Library uses three different types of item identifiers: a bar code for Google-digitized content, a local system identifier for locally digitized content, and an ARK identifier for content originally digitized by the Internet Archive (IA; https://archive.org/).

When requesting the ingestion of a batch of digitized resources, MARCXML metadata are submitted in a single XML file. The `<marc:collection>` element is the root of the XML submitted, and the MARCXML file name is created following the HathiTrust file-naming convention. (The MARCXML schema definition document specifies that `<marc:collection>` may contain one or more child `<marc:record>` elements, meaning that a single file submitted to the HathiTrust may include descriptions of hundreds or even thousands of items ready to be ingested.) Embedded in the file name of the MARCXML submitted to HathiTrust is both a configuration code and a digitizing agent code, as shown in figure 6.1. Each contributing institution can create multiple configuration codes based on its needs. In their processing workflows the Illinois Library uses several configuration codes, including UIUC (for all Illinois content digitized by Google), IA-UIUC (for IA-digitized content), and UIUC-LOC for locally digitized books. These codes are then relied on when creating the institutional prefix used in HathiTrust handles assigned to Illinois-contributed items; for example, one of the prefixes, '`uiug`' for Google books, '`uiuo`' for IA books, and '`uiuc`' for locally digitized books, is embedded in each handle generated for Illinois content contributed to HathiTrust.

HathiTrust has a consistent pattern for creating handles for all ingested digital items. This pattern is depicted in figure 6.2. Whenever a MARCXML metadata file is submitted, the HathiTrust system fetches the item identifier from datafield 955 subfield `$b` from each `<marc:record>` element in the XML. This value is then used when generating HathiTrust handles, appearing

```
<metadata source code>_<configuration code>_<date>_<digitizing
agent>_<other distinguishing  data>.xml
```

Figure 6.1 | **HathiTrust dictates file-naming convention for metadata files submitted**

```
http://hdl.handle.net/2027/<institutionalPrefix>.<item Identifier>
```

Figure 6.2 | **HathiTrust handle consists of a prefix, an institutional prefix, and an item identifier**

in each handle after the HathiTrust handle prefix (http://hdl.handle.net/2027/) and the appropriate institutional prefix (e.g., uiug, uiuo, or uiuc for Illinois items) which is based on the batch's configuration code. This reliable and repeatable pattern allows our workflow at Illinois to anticipate handle values that will be generated for our items during batch ingestion by HathiTrust.

XSLT for adding a HathiTrust handle to MARCXML metadata: The XSLT for updating our local catalog records starts by copying the existing MARCXML record as extracted from the catalog and then adding the HathiTrust handle in datafield 856, which in MARC 21 contains Electronic Location and Access information; for example, a link to an online copy of the resource described. As a first step, the XSLT selects each instance of <marc:record>, using an xsl:for-each element:

```
<xsl:for-each select="/marc:collection/marc:record">
```

This provides an initial road map for the transform. The XSLT then copies everything in each <marc:record> node, using the <xsl:copy-of> element to do so (see figure 6.3). The <marc:record> content model, as defined by the MARCXML schema, allows three child elements; that is, <marc:leader>, <marc:controlfield>, and <marc:datafield>. The XSLT copies all occurrences of these datafields from the original metadata, copying all attributes and child nodes in their entirety.

XSLT instructions are then executed to add the HathiTrust handle into datafield 856. Since the existing metadata extracted from the Illinois catalog describes the print item, the indicators for datafield 856 are set to 4 and 1 respectively. The transform populates two datafield 856 subfields, $3 and $u; the source of the electronic location is added in subfield $3, and the HathiTrust handle is added in subfield $u. Since the source of the electronic location for all records is HathiTrust, the value added to subfield $3 is fixed and hard-coded into the XSLT. To construct the handle value to insert into subfield $u, the XPath function 'concat' is used in conjunction with the <xsl:value-of> element. The three values that need to be concatenated are the HathiTrust handle prefix (http://hdl.handle.net/2027), one of the three institutional prefixes

```
<xsl:copy-of select="marc:leader"/>
<xsl:copy-of select="marc:controlfield"/>
<xsl:copy-of select="marc:datafield"/>
```

Figure 6.3 | **Using <xsl:copy-of> element, the XSLT copies the original MARCXML metadata**

(uiuc, uiuo, or uiug) discussed above, and the datafield 955 subfield $b value (see figure 6.4). Note that ingest batches are homogeneous as to configuration code, so the institutional 'namespace' prefix value is hard-coded into the XSLT and updated as necessary before each batch run.

The complete XSLT that generates the new MARCXML metadata file with the HathiTrust handle added in datafield 856 is shown in figure 6.5. One thing to remember here is that the original XML metadata file has <marc:collection> as its root element. The content model of this element allows it to contain one or more <marc:record> nodes. The transformed MARCXML file maintains the <marc:collection> element as its root and has the same hierarchical structure. Note also that this XSLT imports a utility stylesheet, MARC21slimUtils.xsl, from the Library of Congress. This utility XSLT contains general-purpose templates that are useful when transforming MARCXML catalog records. To improve performance, a copy of this stylesheet may be saved locally and the value of the <xsl:import> element's href attribute changed to a relative (i.e., local) URL. This is also handy if your stylesheet needs to be invoked while not connected to the Web.

```
<datafield tag="856" ind1="4" ind2="1">
       <subfield code="3">
          <xsl:text>Full text - HathiTrust Digital Library</xsl: text>
       </subfield>
       <subfield code="u">
             <xsl:value-of select="concat('http://hdl.handle.net/
2027/uiuc.',marc:datafield[@tag=955]/marc:subfield[@code='b'])"></
xsl:value-of>
       </subfield>
 </datafield>
```

Figure 6.4 | **XSLT adds an 856 <marc:datafield> to the result-tree, populating the element with the source for the web resource (fixed value) and the HathiTrust handle. The value 'uiuc' can be changed to 'uiuo' or 'uiug' depending on the digitization agency.**

```
<?xml version="1.0" encoding="UTF-8" ?>
<xsl:stylesheet version="2.0" xmlns="http://www.loc.gov/MARC21/slim"
    xmlns:marc="http://www.loc.gov/MARC21/slim" xmlns:xsl="http://
    www.w3.org/1999/XSL/Transform"exclude-result-prefixes="marc">
    <xsl:import href="http://www.loc.gov/standards/marcxml/xslt/
    MARC21slimUtils.xsl"/>
    <xsl:output method="xml" encoding="UTF-8" indent="yes"/>
    <xsl:param name="sourcefile"/>
    <xsl:strip-space elements="*"/>
    <xsl:template match="/">
    <collection xmlns="http://www.loc.gov/MARC21/slim"
        xsi:schemaLocation="http://www.loc.gov/MARC21/slim
        http://www.loc.gov/standards/marcxml/schema/MARC21slim.xsd"
        xmlns:xsi="http://www.w3.org/2001/XMLSchema-instance">
        <xsl:for-each select="marc:collection/marc:record">
        <record xmlns="http://www.loc.gov/MARC21/slim"
            xsi:schemaLocation="http://www.loc.gov/MARC21/slim http://
www.loc.gov/standards/marcxml/schema/MARC21slim.xsd"
            xmlns:xsi="http://www.w3.org/2001/XMLSchema-instance">
           <xsl:copy-of select="marc:leader"/>
           <xsl:copy-of select="marc:controlfield"/>
           <xsl:copy-of select="marc:datafield"/>
            <datafield tag="856" ind1="4" ind2="1">
                <subfield code="3">
                    <xsl:text>Full text - HathiTrust Digital
Library</xsl:text>
                </subfield>
                <subfield code="u">
                    <xsl:value-of select="concat('http://hdl.handle.
net/2027/uiuc.',marc:datafield[@tag=955]/marc:subfield[@code='b'])">
                    </xsl:value-of>
                </subfield>
            </datafield>
           </record>
        </xsl:for-each>
    </collection>
   </xsl:template>
 </xsl:stylesheet>
```

Figure 6.5 | **An XSLT for enriching a MARCXML metadata file with HathiTrust handles**

WORKFLOW 2

TRANSFORMING ELECTRONIC THESES AND DISSERTATIONS (ETD) METADATA TO MARC

Background: Since 2010, the University of Illinois at Urbana-Champaign has required graduate students to deposit their theses and dissertations in electronic format. Deposited ETDs are ingested into our institutional repository, IDEALS (https://ideals.illinois.edu/), with most made available to the public immediately (a student can request a release embargo). Initially IDEALS was the only access point for all ETDs produced by Illinois graduates. In IDEALS, the metadata for ETDs is in Dublin Core with additional customized elements; for example, contributor.grantor, contributor.committeeChair, and contributor .committeeMember. The Illinois Library decided to also add metadata for all ETDs into its integrated library system (ILS) so as to preserve institutional memory and provide additional access points from its OPAC and WorldCat. To ingest metadata into our ILS, the IDEALS metadata needed to be transformed into MARCXML. The first step was to create an intellectual mapping from the IDEALS metadata schema to MARC.

Mapping from IDEALS metadata to MARC: Each ETD in IDEALS is linked to a Metadata Encoding and Transmission Standard (METS) file (serialized as XML) that includes not only descriptive metadata but also administrative, technical, structural, and preservation metadata. The descriptive metadata is nested within the `<mets:dmdSec>` element. The XML in figure 6.6 describes the descriptive metadata fields supported. For ETDs in IDEALS, the base descriptive metadata schema used is Dublin Core (`mdschema="dc"`), with qualifiers and custom elements added.

After reviewing the elements used for the descriptive metadata and examining typical values used in practice, a mapping table, as shown in table 6.2, was completed.

Additionally, the transform adds several MARCXML datafields with fixed values as shown in table 6.3. These default values were set based on RDA rules and local cataloging conventions.

XSLT for transforming ETD metadata to MARC: As shown in figure 6.7 (see page 84), the root element of the XSLT for transforming IDEALS-ETD metadata to MARCXML binds each namespace used in the METS file being transformed to a namespace prefix. This is necessary in order to select elements in these namespaces for processing during the transform. Though strictly speaking not required, for convenience and to avoid confusion namespaces are

```xml
<?xml version="1.0" encoding="UTF-8"?>
<dmdSec ID="dmdSec_2">
    <mdWrap MDTYPE="OTHER" OTHERMDTYPE="DIM">
        <xmlData xmlns:dim="http://www.dspace.org/xmlns/dspace/dim">
            <dim:dim xmlns:dim="http://www.dspace.org/xmlns/dspace/dim" dspaceType="ITEM">
                <dim:field mdschema="dc" element="contributor" qualifier="advisor" lang="en_US"/>
                <dim:field mdschema="dc" element="creator" lang="en_US"/>
                <dim:field mdschema="dc" element="date" qualifier="accessioned"/>
                <dim:field mdschema="dc" element="date" qualifier="available"/>
                <dim:field mdschema="dc" element="date" qualifier="created" lang="en_US"/>
                <dim:field mdschema="dc" element="date" qualifier="issued" lang="en_US"/>
                <dim:field mdschema="dc" element="date" qualifier="submitted" lang="en_US"/>
                <dim:field mdschema="dc" element="identifier" qualifier="uri"/>
                <dim:field mdschema="dc" element="description" qualifier="abstract" lang="en_US"/>
                <dim:field mdschema="dc" element="description" qualifier="provenance" lang="en_US"/>
                <dim:field mdschema="dc" element="format" qualifier="mimetype" lang="en_US"/>
                <dim:field mdschema="dc" element="language" qualifier="iso" lang="en_US"/>
                <dim:field mdschema="dc" element="rights" lang="en_US"/>
                <dim:field mdschema="dc" element="subject" lang="en_US"/>
                <dim:field mdschema="dc" element="title" lang="en_US"/>
                <dim:field mdschema="dc" element="type" lang="en_US"/>
                <dim:field mdschema="thesis" element="degree" qualifier="name" lang="en_US"/>
                <dim:field mdschema="thesis" element="degree" qualifier="discipline" lang="en_US"/>
                <dim:field mdschema="thesis" element="degree" qualifier="grantor" lang="en_US"/>
                <dim:field mdschema="thesis" element="degree" qualifier="department" lang="en_US"/>
                <dim:field mdschema="dc" element="contributor" qualifier="committeeChair" lang="en_US"/>
                <dim:field mdschema="dc" element="contributor" qualifier="committeeMember" lang="en_US"/>
                <dim:field mdschema="dc" element="type" qualifier="material" lang="en_US"/>
                <dim:field mdschema="dc" element="description" qualifier="terms"/>
                <dim:field mdschema="dc" element="description" qualifier="reason"/>
                <dim:field mdschema="dc" element="date" qualifier="embargo"/>
            </dim:dim>
        </xmlData>
    </mdWrap>
</dmdSec>
```

Figure 6.6 | **Definition of descriptive metadata fields used in ETD METS file**

Table 6.2 | **Mapping from IDEALS metadata to MARC**

IDEALS METADATA	MARC
mdschema="dc" element="title"	245 1 ? $a
mdschema="dc" element="subject"	653 ## $a
mdschema="dc" element="creator"	100 1# $a
mdschema="dc" element="identifier" qualifier="uri"	856 40 $u
mdschema="dc" element="date" qualifier="created"	264 #1 $c
mdschema="dc" element="date" qualifier="submitted"	008 position 7–10
mdschema="dc" element="description" qualifier="abstract" (take year value only)	505 0# $a
mdschema="thesis" element="degree" qualifier="name"	502 ## $b
mdschema="dc" element="date" qualifier="created" (take year value only)	502 ## $d
mdschema="dc" element="rights"	540 ## $a
mdschema="thesis" element="degree" qualifier="discipline"	690 ## $x
mdschema="dc" element="date" qualifier="created" (take year value only)	690 ## $y

Table 6.3 | **Fixed values that must be added to every MARC record**

DATAFIELD/ INDICATOR	SUBFIELD/VALUE
040 ##	$a UIU $e rda $c UIU
049 ##	$a UIUU $s er
264 #1	$a Urbana, Ill.: $b University of Illinois at Urbana-Champaign;
300 ##	$a 1 PDF file.
336 ##	$a text $2 rdacontent
337 ##	$a computer $2 rdamedia
338 ##	$a online resource $2 rdacarrier
502 ##	$c University of Illinois at Urbana-Champaign
538 ##	$a System requirement: Adobe Acrobat Reader.
538 ##	$a Mode of access: World Wide Web.
690 ##	$a Theses $x UIUC
856 40	$3 Full text—IDEALS

```
<xsl:stylesheet xmlns:xsl="http://www.w3.org/1999/XSL/Transform"
      xmlns:dim="http://www.dspace.org/xmlns/dspace/dim"
      xmlns:xs="http://www.w3.org/2001/XMLSchema"
      xmlns:etd="http://www.ndltd.org/standards/metadata/etdms/1.0/"
      xmlns:mets=http://www.loc.gov/METS/
      xmlns:xd="http://www.oxygenxml.com/ns/doc/xsl"
      exclude-result-prefixes="xs etd  mets" version="2.0">
```

Figure 6.7 | **The XSLT root element binds namespace prefixes appearing in the METS file and excludes unneeded namespace prefixes from the transform result**

```
<controlfield tag="008">151009s<xsl:value-of select="substring(//
dim:field[@element='date' and @qualifier='submitted'],1,4)"/> ilu o 000 0
eng d</controlfield>
```

Figure 6.8 | **XPath `substring` function and `<xsl:value-of>` are used to extract date value (year only) from the IDEALS-ETD metadata record and add it to `<marc:controlfield>` 008, positions 7–10**

bound in the XSLT to the same namespace prefixes used in the METS file, for example, `mets`, `dim`, `etd`, and so on. The `exclude-result-prefixes` attribute is also included on the XSLT root element in order to list namespace bindings that can be excluded (are no longer needed) once the transform has been performed.

One of the first steps of the transform adds the `<marc:leader>` element and the 006 and 007 `<marc:controlfield>` elements, populating each with fixed (default) values that are the same for all ETD descriptions. For the 008 `<marc:controlfield>` element, most of the content is fixed; only the date information in positions 7–10 of the content is modified based on the value in the IDEALS-ETD metadata record being transformed. As shown in figure 6.8, this is done using the XPath `substring` function and the `<xsl:value-of>` element. The IDEALS-ETD date format supports various date granularity up to and including year-month-day time. The XPath substring function is used to extract only the four-digit year information contained in the first four characters of the IDEALS-ETD `date.submitted` string value. Month, day, and time information, if present, is ignored.

Transformations of the remaining fields in the IDEALS-ETD source metadata record generally fall into one of the following three categories:

1. Simple one-to-one mappings; source-tree field value is added to the result-tree unmodified;

```
<xsl:for-each select="//dim:field">
      <xsl:iftest="./@element='description' and./@qualifier='abstract'">
            <datafield tag="520" ind1="0" ind2=" ">
                  <subfield code="a">
                        <xsl:value-of select="."/>
                  </subfield>
            </datafield>
      </xsl:if>
</xsl:for-each>
```

Figure 6.9 | **When source-tree value does not need to be modified, the value can be used without change to populate the appropriate MARCXML datafield and subfield in the result-tree**

2. Source field values need to be modified before being added to the result-tree; and
3. Fixed (default) values, the same for all Illinois ETDs, are added to the result-tree.

Transformations 1 and 2 are handled using the `<xsl:for-each>` and `<xsl:value-of>` elements. The `<xsl:if>` element is also used to check whether the element is present in the IDEALS-ETD metadata record (i.e., the source-tree). When present and the mapping is one-to-one (the first class of transformation listed), that is, when the value comes from only one IDEALS-ETD metadata field and there is no requirement to modify or reformat the value, it is simple to transform the source-tree metadata into the appropriate MARC datafield in the result-tree. For example, values found in the IDEALS-ETD description.abstract field can be used to populate the 520 `<marc:datafield>` subfield `$a` by using `<xsl:for-each>`, `<xsl:if>`, and `<xsl:value-of>` with an attribute of `select='.'`, as shown in figure 6.9. This XSLT snippet uses the value in the description.abstract field to populate a 520 `<marc:datafield>` and then add it to the result-tree. In the absence of description.abstract in the source-tree, the 520 `<marc:datafield>` will be omitted from the result-tree as well.

There are some datafields that require conditional transformation. For example, MARC datafields 100, 245, and 700 need different indicators and values depending on values found in the IDEALS-ETD metadata. Values used in the 100 `<marc:datafield>` (Main Entry-Personal Name) must be terminated by a period. While reviewing by hand a sampling of metadata records, it was noticed that in the IDEALS-ETD records some names have a period and some names do not. XSLT can check for the existence of the period in source-tree values and add the punctuation when it is not there, or take the value as is when the period is present, by using the elements `<xsl:choose>`, `<xsl:when>`, and `<xsl:otherwise>`. Figure 6.10 illustrates how this is done in XSLT. When the IDEALS-ETD creator value ends with a period (`test="ends-with(., '.')"`), then the source-tree value is used unchanged to populate the 100 `<marc:datafield>` that is added to the result-tree. Otherwise, the value from the source-tree is modified, adding a period before populating the 100 `<marc:datafield>` in the result-tree.

The same conditional XSLT elements can be used to determine the 245 `<marc:datafield>` indicators as they are added to the result-tree. Since the value of the second indicator represents the number of nonfiling characters (the first indicator is always '`1`' because all ETDs have authors), the XSLT can use the XPath `starts-with` function to check the start of the source-tree title string value and determine the number of nonfiling characters. For example, when the string starts with 'The' (`xsl:when test="starts-with(./.,'The')"`), the second indicator should be '`4`' as shown in figure 6.11. When no nonfiling characters are recognized, then the second indicator will be '`0`'.

```
<xsl:for-each select="//dim:field">
    <xsl:if test="./@element='creator'">
        <xsl:choose>
            <xsl:when test="ends-with(.,'.')">
                <datafield tag="100" ind1="1" ind2=" ">
                        <subfield code="a">
                                <xsl:value-of select="."/>
                        </subfield>
                </datafield>
            </xsl:when>
            <xsl:otherwise>
                <datafield tag="100" ind1="1" ind2=" ">
                        <subfield code="a"><xsl:value-of select="."/>.</
                        subfield>
                </datafield>
            </xsl:otherwise>
        </xsl:choose>
    </xsl:if>
</xsl:for-each>
```

Figure 6.10 | **Checking whether the source-tree value ends with a period or not ensures that all values in 100 `<marc:datafield>` that are added to the result-tree will end with a period**

Elements populated with fixed values are most easily added to the result-tree as literal result elements, as illustrated in figure 6.12.

XSLT can help to make cataloging workflows efficient and productive. However, in order to design an efficient XSLT, it is essential to start with accurate, high-quality metadata and understand not only the semantics of XSLT and XPath, but also understand local and national cataloging practices, content standards, and the semantics of different metadata schemas.

```
<xsl:for-each select=”//dim:field”>
    <xsl:if test=”./@element=’title’”>
        <xsl:choose>
            <xsl:when test=”starts-with(./.,’The ‘)”>
                <datafield tag=”245” ind1=”1” ind2=”4”>
                    <subfield code=”a”><xsl:value-of select=”.”/>.</
                    subfield>
                </datafield>
            </xsl:when>
            <xsl:when test=”starts-with(./.,’An ‘)”>
                <datafield tag=”245” ind1=”1” ind2=”3”>
                    <subfield code=”a”><xsl:value-of select=”.”/>.</
                    subfield>
                </datafield>
            </xsl:when>
            <xsl:when test=”starts-with(./.,’A ‘)”>
                <datafield tag=”245” ind1=”1” ind2=”2”>
                    <subfield code=”a”><xsl:value-of select=”.”/>.</
                    subfield>
                </datafield>
            </xsl:when>
            <xsl:otherwise>
                <datafield tag=”245” ind1=”1” ind2=”0”>
                    <subfield code=”a”><xsl:value-of select=”.”/>.</
                    subfield>
                </datafield>
            </xsl:otherwise>
        </xsl:choose>
    </xsl:if>
</xsl:for-each>
```

igure 6.11 | **The second indicator value of the datafield 245 can be determined using `<xsl:choose>` and the XPath `starts-with` function**

```
<datafield tag="300" ind1=" " ind2=" ">
        <subfield code="a">1 online resource (1 PDF file)</subfield>
</datafield>

<datafield tag="336" ind1=" " ind2=" ">
        <subfield code="a">text</subfield>
        <subfield code="b">txt</subfield>
        <subfield code="2">rdacontent</subfield>
</datafield>

<datafield tag="337" ind1=" " ind2=" ">
        <subfield code="a">computer</subfield>
        <subfield code="b">c</subfield>
        <subfield code="2">rdamedia</subfield>
</datafield>

<datafield tag="338" ind1=" " ind2=" ">
        <subfield code="a">online resource</subfield>
        <subfield code="b">cr</subfield>
        <subfield code="2">rdacarrier</subfield>
</datafield>
```

Figure 6.12 | **Elements with fixed values are added to the result-tree as literal result elements**

USING XSLT TO CONNECT LIBRARIES TO THE SEMANTIC WEB

Transforming XML Metadata into HTML+RDFa

Libraries are exploring the use of the semantic web and linked open data (LOD) as a way to make their rich and unique resources more discoverable and useful on the Web. Fundamental to all implementations of LOD is the use of the Resource Description Framework (RDF) to describe the resources that are being shared and linked into the semantic web. RDF models the description of any resource as a set of simple statements pertaining to that resource; for example, book A has the title "Moby Dick," Herman Melville is the author of book A, chapter 5 is part of book A, chapter 5 has the title "Breakfast," and so on. Each of these statements consists of a subject (book A, Herman Melville, chapter 5), a predicate/property (has the title, is the author of, is part of), and an object ("Moby Dick," book A, "Breakfast"). As its name implies, RDF provides the syntax and semantics for expressing such simple statements, but it does not provide the semantics, that is, the domain-specific predicate values and classes of subjects and objects that make these descriptions useful. Content provider and developer communities create such semantics to meet the needs of their users. Web search engine developers (e.g., Google, Microsoft, Yahoo!, Yandex) have collaboratively developed schema.org (http://schema.org/), one such set of semantics for use with RDF.

The semantics of schema.org have emerged as one of the easiest and simplest ways to publish library metadata as linked open data on the Web.

RDF can be serialized in a number of formats, including XML, but since RDF is designed especially to describe resources present on the Web, one popular approach is to embed RDF descriptions within HTML documents using RDF in Attributes (RDFa; https://rdfa.info/). In RDFa, attributes are used to embellish an HTML document, identifying statement subjects, objects, and predicates. Assuming that the prefix 'schema:' had been bound elsewhere in the HTML document to the namespace URI: http://schema.org, and assuming that the digital copy of *Moby Dick* being described was available from www.literaturepage.com/read/mobydick.html, the following snippet of HTML conveys the name (aka title) of the book being described in RDFa:

```
<h2 resource="http://www.literaturepage.com/read/
mobydick.html" property="schema:name">Moby Dick</
resource>
```

Note that the object of the statement, the string "Moby Dick," is the content of the h2 element. The subject of the statement is the value of the `resource` attribute, and the predicate of the statement is the value of the `property` attribute. One attraction of RDFa is that the same HTML document can both display information about a library resource to human library users and provide machine-processable descriptions of that same resource.

The library of the University of Illinois at Urbana-Champaign has experimented with RDF and RDFa over the course of several recent research projects, including one project that led to the publication of a snapshot of all of the Illinois Library's catalog records as linked open data.[1] XSLT already is often used to transform XML metadata records into HTML for presentation to library users. Now XSLT is proving quite useful in transforming library metadata into HTML+RDFa. This chapter describes an XSLT that transforms XML metadata into HTML+RDFa for the Emblematica Online project (http://emblematica.library.illinois.edu/).[2]

EMBLEMATICA ONLINE AND ITS METADATA

The Early Modern emblem book was a popular literary genre in Europe from the mid-sixteenth through the mid-eighteenth centuries. Not surprisingly, emblem books contain emblems (which also appeared in applied settings, e.g., in church architecture, as decorations on ceramics, etc.). Each emblem book contains anywhere from a handful of emblems to well over a thousand emblems. The emblem format is compound, integrating text and graphics. The exact structure of emblems varies, but most include an image element (the *pictura*), a short motto textual element (the *inscriptio*), and a longer verse textual element (the *subscriptio*). Printed emblems can be anywhere from a single page to more than twenty pages in length.

Emblematica Online (http://emblematica.library.illinois.edu) is a portal for digitized print emblem resources that integrates notable emblem book collections from six libraries around the world: the University of Illinois at Urbana-Champaign, the Herzog August Bibliothek Wolfenbüttel, Glasgow University, Utrecht University, the Getty Research Institute, and Duke University. As of this writing, the portal provides discovery and access to approximately 1,400 digitized emblem books and a 28,500 count subset of the emblems contained in these books.

Scholars need to discover and access emblem books both at the book level (i.e., searching over book bibliographic information) and at the granularity of the individual emblem (e.g., searching over mottos and *pictura* descriptors). Figure 7.1 is a screenshot of an emblem book description from the Emblematica Online portal, while figure 7.2 is a screenshot of a single emblem description with links to higher-resolution views. Varying granular levels of discovery are possible because digitized emblem resources are described using the SPINE metadata schema. Developed in 2004, the SPINE schema is used widely in the emblem community because it allows for descriptions of the digitized book, copy information, and emblems (from the book) all in a single record.[3] An XML schema definition (XSD) was created and is maintained by the Herzog August Bibliothek (http://diglib.hab.de/rules/schema/emblem/emblem-1–2.xsd).

To describe a digitized emblem book, the SPINE schema allows the use of either the Metadata Object Description Schema (MODS; www.loc.gov/standards/mods/) semantics or the Text Encoding Initiative (TEI) Header (www.tei-c.org/release/doc/tei-p5-doc/en/html/HD.html) semantics. These two metadata schemas are widely used in the library domain (MODS) and by humanities scholars (TEI Header) to describe book-like resources, and descriptions already exist for most emblem books in one or the other of these schema. There are also consensus XSLTs available to transform traditional MARC catalog records into MODS and TEI Header. For the copy description, the SPINE schema uses an element from its own namespace, `<copyDesc>`. The content model for the element `<copyDesc>` includes sub-elements to

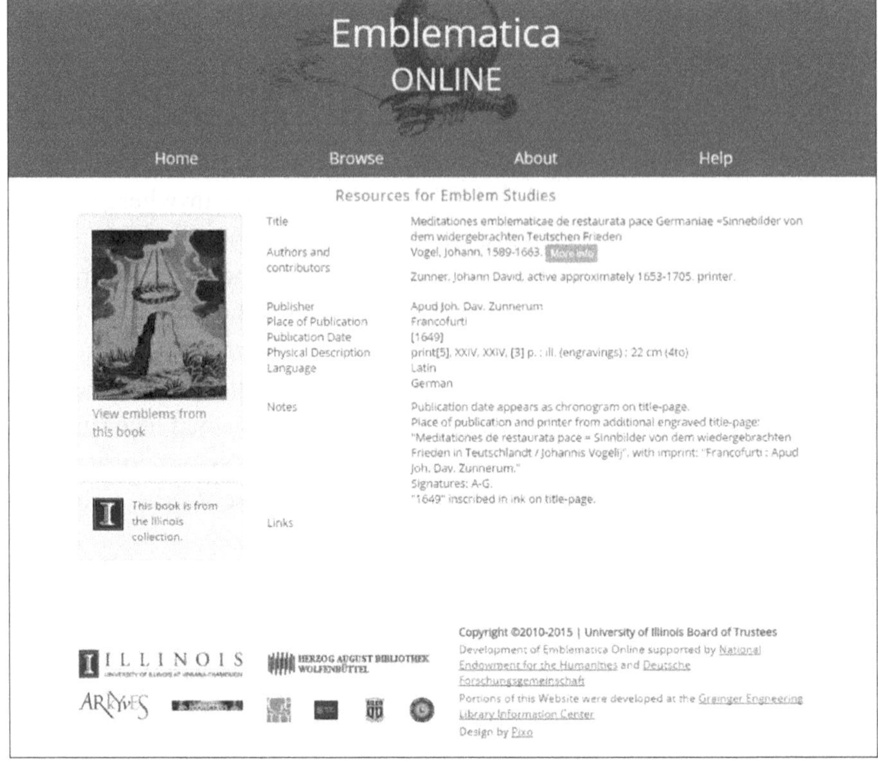

Figure 7.1 | **Screenshot of an emblem book description (from Emblematica Online)**

describe information about the copy of an emblem book actually digitized and the digitization outcome. The SPINE elements <copyID>, <owner>, and <digDesc> are used for describing the digital instance resulting from the digitization. Finally, to describe each emblem contained in a book, a SPINE <emblem> element is provided, along with sub-elements supporting the description of different emblem components, including <motto> for the title of the emblem (transcribed, normalized, and/or translated into different languages), <pictura> for the image of the emblem, and <subscriptio> for the textual part of the emblem. Each of these emblem subcomponents offers another potential access point for discovery.

As a first experiment and in order to facilitate web search engine indexing of the digitized emblem resources available in the Emblematica Online portal, researchers at the University of Illinois at Urbana-Champaign and the Herzog August Bibliothek in Germany decided to enhance the portal's web page with RDFa embedded HTML pages using schema.org semantics. As mentioned, schema.org was developed by major search engines, including Google and Bing,

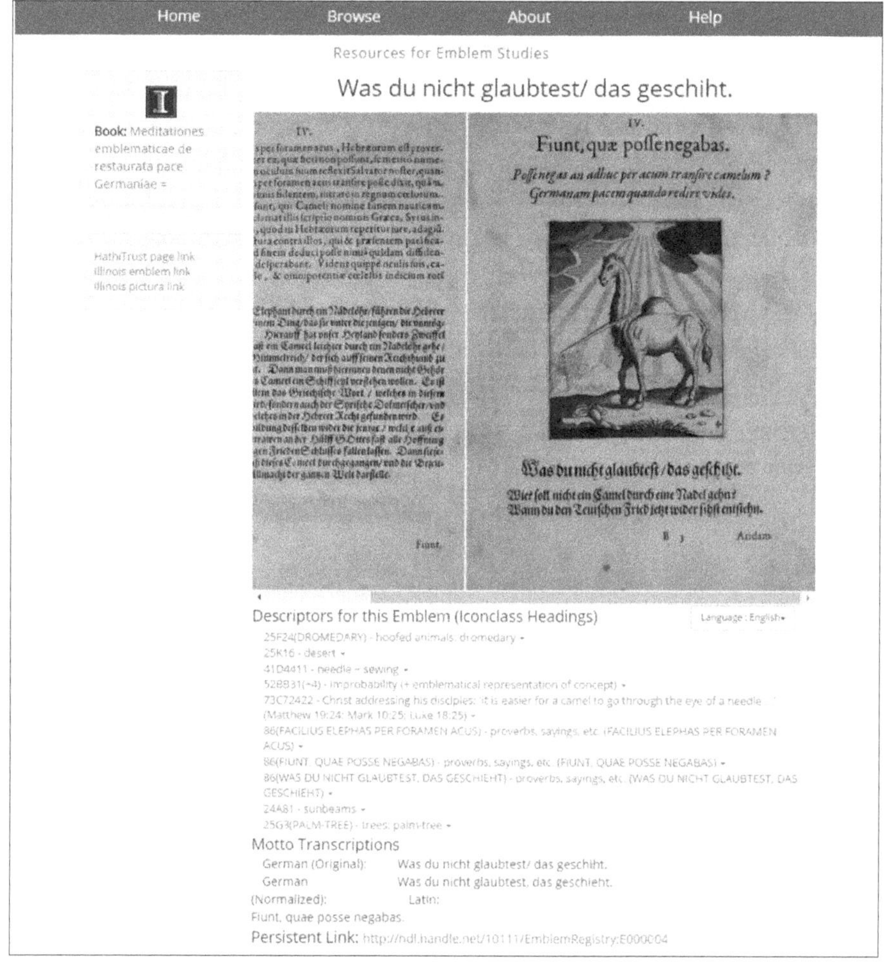

Figure 7.2 | **Screenshot of a single emblem description (from Emblematica Online)**

for just this purpose. SPINE records are maintained in Emblematica Online in XML, making transformation to HTML+RDFa by XSLT a natural choice.

MAPPING SPINE METADATA TO SCHEMA.ORG

The first step to transform SPINE metadata to HTML+RDFa is mapping SPINE metadata semantics to schema.org semantics. Researchers examined schema.org types and properties to determine if they could fully match them to the elements in SPINE. For this process, the SPINE metadata structure was divided into three parts: the book description in MODS, the description of the copy or copies digitized, and the emblem descriptions. The mapping process revealed which SPINE metadata elements match schema.org semantics, can be mapped to similar/appropriate schema.org semantics, or have no analogous semantics in schema.org. For the last mapping category, no (or very poor) alignment, extensions to schema.org semantics were required (e: namespace).

Mapping for book and copy information: Mapping book bibliographic descriptions to schema.org turns out to be relatively easy since schema:Book is already a class in schema.org (a subclass of schema:CreativeWork), as shown in table 7.1. Most of the MODS properties and classes have an analogue among schema.org properties and classes. Since currently all book-level metadata in Emblematica

Table 7.1 | **MODS to schema.org mapping. Most of the MODS elements have matching semantics in schema.org**

MODS	SCHEMA.ORG
mods:name	Book > author
mods:titleInfo	Book > name Book > alternateName
mods:originInfo > mods:place	Book > publisher > Organization > location
mods:originInfo > mods:publisher	Book > publisher
mods:originInfo > mods:name@role= “printer”	Book > contributor @role=”prt”
mods:originInfo > mods:dateIssued	Book > datePublished
mods:originfo > mods:edition mods:originInfo > mods:dateCaptured ... > mods:publisher > ‘HAB Wolfenbüttel’ ... > mods:.edition > ‘[Electronic Edition]’	Book > bookEdition Product > productionDate Product > manufacturer > Organization > name Product > additionalType > e:DigitizationSource
mods:language	Book > inLanguage > Language
mods:name	Book > contributor ->hasRole
mods:note	Book > description
mods:genre	Book > genre > { Text or URL }
mods:subject	Book > about > e:ConceptCode > codingSystem > codeValue > name > url or sameAs > hasPart
mods:physicalDescription > extent	Book > description and/or Book > numberOfPages
mods:physicalDescription > digitalOrigin mods:physicalDescription > form	Product > additionalType > e:DigitizationSource N / A

Online is maintained in MODS (rather than TEI Header), the mapping from MODS to schema.org (as detailed in table 7.1) was easy to implement.

Mapping from the SPINE `<copyDesc>` element to schema.org is also straightforward (see table 7.2). Since the information included in the `<copyDesc>` element is similar to library holdings and item information, the schema .org Product class and the associated offers property were utilized. One exception is the attribute `comp` in SPINE, describing whether the digitization is complete or not. Since there is no analogous property in schema.org, a new property `<isComplete>` was added to the provisional emblem-specific extension of schema.org to accommodate this information.

Mapping for emblem information: Mapping the emblem description section of SPINE metadata records was not as simple, as apparent from table 7.3. Since the emblem is a rarer type of resource, schema.org does not have all the needed properties and classes. The community that developed schema.org anticipated the potential for this kind of limitation and so provided an ontology extension mechanism. The approach taken for this workflow was to use as many existing schema.org properties as possible, and then add a limited number of classes and properties as extensions to handle essential emblem-related descriptive needs. This is a much better solution than creating a whole new ontology and is in the same spirit as metadata application profiles, long-established within the library community.[4]

Table 7.2 | **Mapping SPINE <copyDesc> content model to schema.org**

COPY INFORMATION	SCHEMA.ORG
copyDesc > digDesc	Product > description Product > offers > Offer > description
copyDesc > digDesc > @comp	Product > e:isComplete (Boolean) Product > offers > Offer > e:isComplete (Boolean)
copyDesc > digDesc > copyID copyDesc > digDesc > @globalID copyDesc > copyID	Book > offers > Offer > sku *(if needed for non-URL ids)* Book > offers > Offer > url (preferred) Product > isConsumableFor > Product/CW > sku Product > isConsumableFor > Product/CW > sameAs (use this for the OCLC id of print book digitized)
copyDesc > digDesc > owner copyDesc > owner	Book > offers > Offer > offeredBy > Organization Product > isConsumableFor > Product/CW > provider > Organization
owner > @countryCode	Organization > location > Place > url or sameAs > name

Table 7.3 | **<emblem> to schema.org emblem extension mapping**

EMBLEM INFORMATION	SCHEMA.ORG -> PROPOSED EMBLEM EXTENSION (E:)
emblem>@id	e:Emblem > e:additionalID > name > value > propertyID
emblem> @xlink:href	e:Emblem > url
N / A	e:Emblem > b:pageStart / b:pageEnd OR e:Emblem > b:pagination
emblem> @citeNo	e:Emblem > citeNo
emblem> @standNo	e:Emblem > standardNo
emblem>dedication	e:Emblem > e:Dedication > CreativeWork > text (e:Dedication is a CreativeWork)
emblem>sectionTitle	e:Book > hasPart > b:Collection e:Book > hasPart > b:Collection > inLanguage (needed here to provide the language of the Section title / sub-section title)
emblem>sectionTitle	b:Collection > name
emblem>sectionTitle @type	b:Collection > alternateName (use only for a name version normalized in modern spelling/ grammar of original language)
emblem>sectionTitle @type	b:Collection > e:translationOfName > inLanguage > text > b:translator (i.e., e:translationOfName is a CreativeWork)
N / A	b:Collection > hasPart > b:Collection . . . (follow pattern of 9 A – C)
N / A	b:Collection > hasPart > b:Collection . . . (follow pattern of 9 A – C)
N / A	b:Collection > hasPart > b:Collection . . . (follow pattern of 9 A – C)
emblem>reference (use type of reference)	e:Emblem > isBasedOnUrl OR e:Emblem > citation OR e:Emblem > mentions
emblem>reference (use type of reference)	e:Emblem > e:editorialReference (object is Text or CreativeWork)
emblem>relationship> derivation	e:Emblem > isBasedOnUrl e:Emblem > e:reusedIn > { URL or Text }
emblem>relationship	N / A
emblem>note	e:Emblem > description
emblem>note	e:Emblem > comment
emblem>motif	e:Emblem > e:textualMotif

EMBLEM INFORMATION	SCHEMA.ORG -> PROPOSED EMBLEM EXTENSION (E:)
emblem>motif	e:Emblem > e:pictorialMotif
emblem>topic	e:Emblem > keywords (delimit by commas)
emblem>theme	e:Emblem > keywords (delimit by commas)
emblem>iconclass emblem>keyword	e: Emblem > about > e:ConceptCode > codingSystem > codeValue > name > url or sameAs > hasPart
N / A	e:EmblemPictura > b:artist > Person
emblem>@medium	e:EmblemPictura > artMedium
emblem>emblemParts	e:EmblemTextPart > additionalType > { e:Motto, e:Subscriptio, e:Commentatio }
Transcription	e:EmblemTextPart > text > inLanguage
Normalization	e:EmblemTextPart > e:alternateText
Respective emblemPart	e:EmblemTextPart > b:translationOfWork > text > inLanguage > b:translator
source (@type)	e:EmblemTextPart > keywords
Source	e:EmblemTextPart > isBasedOnUrl OR e:EmblemTextPart > citation OR e:EmblemTextPart > mentions OR
source (@type)	e:EmblemTextPart > e:editorialReference
@statedOriginal	e:EmblemTextPart > e:meterFromOriginal
N / A	e:EmblemTextPart > e:meterAddedEditorially

XSLT TO TRANSFORM SPINE XML METADATA TO HTML+RDFA

Since the Emblematica Online portal has two display pages, one for book-level display and the other for emblem-level, two XSLTs were created. One generates the book-level HTML+RDFa and the other produces the emblem-level HTML+RDFa. However, these two XSLTs share some features. For example, since both book-level and emblem-level information are present in SPINE records, both XSLTs share most of the same namespace bindings, as shown in figure 7.3.

```
xmlns:xsl="http://www.w3.org/1999/XSL/Transform"
xmlns:xsi="http://www.w3.org/2001/XMLSchema-instance"
xmlns:html="http://www.w3.org/1999/xhtml"
xmlns:xlink="http://www.w3.org/1999/xlink" version="1.0"
xmlns:spine=http://diglib.hab.de/rules/schema/emblem
```

Figure 7.3 | **Namespace bindings shared by both book-level and emblem-level XSLTs**

Table 7.4 | **Display labels for schema.org properties**

SCHEMA.ORG PROPERTY	DISPLAY NAME
<Product><name>	Title
<Book> <author><name><jobTitle> <contributor>< name><jobTitle>	Authors and contributors
<publisher><name>	Publisher
<Place><locationCreated>	Place of Publication
<datePublished>	Publication Date
<description>	Physical Description
<Language><inLanguage>	Language
<about>	Subjects
<description>	Notes

Generating book-level HTML+RDFa: In addition to mapping from MODS to schema.org, a new mapping to HTML was also developed. This mapping was concerned with how best to organize and present metadata to human users of Emblematica Online, whereas the mappings to schema.org semantics focused on transforming MODS metadata optimally for web harvesters. The HTML mapping process considered display labels as well as mappings to HTML elements and attributes. Table 7.4 outlines the labels used in HTML for each schema.org property.

In addition to the namespace bindings shown in figure 7.3, the root element for the book display XSLT included one additional namespace binding for the MODS namespace: `xmlns:mods="http://www.loc.gov/mods/v3"`. As mentioned, six different libraries contributed metadata to Emblematica Online. Participating libraries understand MODS semantics in slightly different ways, resulting in some inconsistencies in where information like the best link to the digitized emblem book being described appears in the MODS record. For the

```
<xsl:variable name="BookUri">
    <xsl:choose>
      <xsl:when test="/spine:biblioDesc/mods:mods/mods:location/
mods:url/@usage='primary display' ">
        <xsl:value-of
          select="/spine:biblioDesc/mods:mods/mods:location/mods:url[@
usage='primary display']"/>
      </xsl:when>
      <xsl:when test="//mods:mods/mods:identifier/@type='purl' ">
        <xsl:value-of select="//mods:mods/mods:identifier[@
type='purl']"/>
      </xsl:when>
      <xsl:when test="//mods:mods/mods:location/mods:url">
        <xsl:value-of select="//mods:mods/mods:location/mods:url"/>
      </xsl:when>
    </xsl:choose>
  </xsl:variable>
```

igure 7.4 | **Defining variable values in an XSLT**

book-level XSLT, the second child of the `<xsl:stylesheet>` root element (i.e., following the `<xsl:output>` element and before any `<xsl:template>` elements) is `<xsl:variable>`. This `<xsl:variable>` element declares and sets the value of the global variable `$BookUri`. The value of this variable is set using an `<xsl:choose>` instruction containing an ordered series of three test XPath expressions (see figure 7.4). Each of these expressions is evaluated in order until a matching element (true test result) is found in the source-tree. The value of the matching element is then used to set the value of the `$BookUri` variable and any test expressions in the `<xsl:choose>` not yet evaluated are skipped. If none of the three expressions yield a match, then the value of `$BookUri` is left empty. The first expression checks the source-tree for a `<mods:location>` element containing a `<mods:url>` element having a `usage='primary display'` attribute. The second expression checks for a `<mods:identifier>` element having a `type='purl'` attribute. The third expression checks for a `<mods:location>` element containing a `<mods:url>` element. This selection tree reflects the range of different ways in the MODS metadata that links to digitized emblem books appear.

An `<xsl:template>` element matching on the document node is next after the `$BookUri` variable has been set. This template adds `<html>` and `<head>` elements to the result-tree along with the `<body>` element start

```
<div class="table" prefix="s: http://schema.org/
        e: http://emblematica.library.illinois.edu/schemas/emb/"
    typeof="s:Book" resource="{$BookUri}">
    <meta property="s:additionalType"
content="http://schema.org/Product"/>
```

Figure 7.5 | **Add namespace prefixes and other RDFa attributes and values to the result-tree**

```
<div class="row">
        <div class="col-sm-3">
          <span>
            <b>Title</b>
          </span>
        </div>
        <div class="col-sm-9">
          <span property="s:name">
            <xsl:value-of select="mods:titleInfo/mods:title"/>
            <xsl:value-of select="mods:titleInfo/mods:subTitle"/>
          </span>
        </div>
</div>
```

Figure 7.6 | **Create HTML <div> and <span> elements to display book title and simultaneously provide value of <schema:name> property; populate with values from <mods:titleInfo>**

tag. The remaining templates in the XSLT are then applied to the top-level `<mods:mods>` element in the Spine record being transformed. These templates add content, HTML `<div>`, `<span>`, `<meta>`, and `<ul>` elements, and RDFa attributes to the result-tree. The first `<div>` element includes an RDFa attribute, `prefix`, to bind namespace URIs to prefixes. A `class` attribute with the value `table` is also included to facilitate the CSS-based styling of the HTML display. The RDFa attributes `typeof` and `resource` are also included to establish that the description contained in the result HTML is of the schema.org Book class and to provide the URI (i.e., the value of `$BookUri`) for the book being described. In order to describe copy-specific information, an additional class, schema.org `Product` is also assigned. This is done using an empty HTML `<meta>` element. The first `<div>`element and its first child (a `<meta>` element) are shown in figure 7.5.

Subsequent property values from the MODS metadata are added to the result-tree by subsequent `<xsl:template>` elements. Each `<div>` in the

```
<div class="row">
    <div class="col-sm-3">
       <span>
           <b>Title</b>
       </span>
    </div>
    <div class="col-sm-9">
      <span property="s:name">Meditationes emblematicae de restaurata
pace Germaniae =Sinnebilder von dem widergebrachten Teutschen
Frieden</span>
    </div>
</div>
```

Figure 7.7 | **Result of the XSLT snippet shown in figure 7.6**

result-tree represents a row with a label (see table 7.4), a specific schema.org property, and a value or values from the corresponding MODS element(s). For example, the `<div>` element displaying book title information maps two matching MODS elements, `<mods:title>` and `<mods:subTitle>`, (both of which are found in the `<mods:titleInfo>` element), to the `<schema:name>` property. The MODS values are selected using `<xsl:value-of>`, as shown in figure 7.6. Figure 7.7 shows a typical result of the snippet of XSLT provided in figure 7.6. The complete book-level XSLT is provided in appendix B.

Emblem-level HTML page: The emblem-level XSLT transforms each `<emblem>` node in a source SPINE metadata record into an HTML `<div>` element designed to display the key components of the emblem description, for example, Iconclass descriptors and motto transcriptions, to users, while simultaneously populating the RDFa, schema.org description of each emblem. This XSLT binds an additional namespace for SKOS:

```
xmlns:skos="http://www.w3.org/2004/02/skos/core#"
```

The SKOS namespace is used in SPINE emblem nodes when describing Iconclass descriptors that have been assigned to the emblem. Again, the top-level HTML `<div>` element added to the result-tree by the XSLT binds namespace prefixes and populates the RDFa `typeof` attribute, as shown in figure 7.8. In this case, however, there is no need for a global variable analogous to `$BookUri` as used for the book-level XSLT. The URI for the emblem is consistently the value of the `globalID` attribute of each SPINE `<emblem>` element. Note also that in the emblem-level XSLT the RDFa `resource` attribute is added to the result-tree using an `<xsl:attribute>` element, as shown in figure 7.8.

```
<div class="table" prefix="s: http://schema.org/
       e: http://emblematica.library.illinois.edu/schemas/emb/"
     typeof="s:CreativeWork">
   <xsl:attribute name="resource">
      <xsl:value-of select="@globalID"/>
   </xsl:attribute>
```

Figure 7.8 | **Use RDFa attributes to define namespace prefixes and schema.org class of emblem**

For the Iconclass headings, the XSLT checks first for the presence of Iconclass descriptors in each <emblem> node by checking the count of the SPINE <iconclass> element(s) appearing within an <emblem> node. It does this using the XPath <count> function. As shown in the <xsl:when> at the top of figure 7.9, if the count of <iconclass> elements is zero, then the text, "No available descriptors for this emblem (Iconclass Headings)" is added to the result-tree and the sequence constructor in the <xsl:otherwise> element is skipped.

When the count of <iconclass> elements is greater than zero, the <xsl:otherwise> sequence constructor is applied. The list of all Iconclass headings assigned to the emblem is transformed into HTML (one HTML <p> element is generated per Iconclass heading) and displayed under the label "Descriptors for this Emblem (Iconclass Headings)." Using the <xsl:attribute> instruction, each Iconclass heading is simultaneously mapped to <schema:about>. This is accomplished by adding an RDFa property attribute to each HTML <p> element. Additional XSLT instructions and XPath functions construct the URL link to each Iconclass heading, which then appears as the value of the RDFa resource attribute added to each HTML <p> element. The result of this part of the transform can be seen in figure 7.10, which shows a list of Iconclass headings transformed into HTML+RDFa in accordance with the sequence constructor contained in the <xsl:otherwise> element shown in figure 7.9. The complete XSLT used for generating the emblem-level HTML+RDFa is provided in appendix C.

Of course, RDFa is only useful if harvesters and others on the Web make use of it. Google provides a tool that extracts RDFa from web pages and displays it to developers so that they can check for errors and determine if their RDFa is being understood and translated into RDF statements as expected. Figure 7.11 shows how the RDFa generated by the book-level XSLT described above (in left pane) looks when parsed by Google's Structured Data Testing Tool

```
<xsl:choose>
   <xsl:when test="count(emblem:pictura/emblem:iconclass) = 0">
      <div class="col-sm-12">
        <span class="font-20">No available descriptors for this emblem
(Iconclass Headings)</span>
      </div>
   </xsl:when>
   <xsl:otherwise>
      <div id="label" class="col-sm-9">
         <span class="font-20">Descriptors for this Emblem (Iconclass
Headings)</span>
      </div>
     <xsl:for-each select="emblem:pictura/emblem:iconclass">
          <xsl:element name="p">
             <xsl:attribute name="class">iconclass</xsl:attribute>
             <xsl:attribute name="property">s:about</xsl:attribute>
             <xsl:attribute name="id">
                <xsl:value-of select="concat('iconclass-', position())"/>
             </xsl:attribute>
             <xsl:variable name="uriEncodedOpenParenthesis">
                <xsl:call-template name="string-replace-all">
                   <xsl:with-param name="text" select="skos:notation" />
                   <xsl:with-param name="replace">(</xsl:with-param>
                   <xsl:with-param name="by">%28</xsl:with-param>
                </xsl:call-template>
             </xsl:variable>
             <xsl:variable name="uriEncodedCloseParenthesis">
                <xsl:call-template name="string-replace-all">
                   <xsl:with-param name="text"
select="$uriEncodedOpenParenthesis" />
                   <xsl:with-param name="replace">)</xsl:with-param>
                   <xsl:with-param name="by">%29</xsl:with-param>
                </xsl:call-template>
             </xsl:variable>
             <xsl:variable name="uriEncodedNotation">
                <xsl:call-template name="string-replace-all">
                   <xsl:with-param name="text"
select="$uriEncodedCloseParenthesis" />
                   <xsl:with-param name="replace" xml:space="preserve">
                   </xsl:with-param>
                   <xsl:with-param name="by">%20</xsl:with-param>
                </xsl:call-template>
             </xsl:variable>
             <xsl:attribute name="resource"><xsl:value-of
select="concat('http://iconclass.org/',$uriEncodedNotation)"/></
xsl:attribute>
                <xsl:value-of select="skos:notation"/>
          </xsl:element>
      </xsl:for-each>
   </xsl:otherwise>
</xsl:choose>
```

Figure 7.9 | **A portion of the XSLT that creates HTML for Iconclass headings**

```
<div class="col-sm-3 label">
   <span class="font-20">Descriptors for this Emblem (Iconclass
Headings)</span>
</div>
<div class="col-sm-9">
   <p class="iconclass"
      property="s:about"
      id="iconclass-1"
      resource="http://iconclass.org/22C11">22C11</p>
   <p class="iconclass"
      property="s:about"
      id="iconclass-2"
      resource="http://iconclass.org/25H1124">25H1124</p>
   <p class="iconclass"
      property="s:about"
      id="iconclass-3"
      resource="http://iconclass.org/45A20">45A20</p>
   <p class="iconclass"
      property="s:about"
      id="iconclass-4"
      resource="http://iconclass.org/61A%28...%29">61A(...)</p>
   <p class="iconclass"
      property="s:about"
      id="iconclass-5"
      resource="http://iconclass.org/61K%28...%29">61K(...)</p>
   <p class="iconclass"
      property="s:about"
      id="iconclass-6"
      resource="http://iconclass.org/86%28...%29">86(...)</p>
   <p class="iconclass"
      property="s:about"
      id="iconclass-7"
      resource="http://iconclass.org/86%28...%29%20">86(...) </p>
   <p class="iconclass"
      property="s:about"
      id="iconclass-8"
      resource="http://iconclass.org/96A16">96A16</p>
</div>
```

Figure 7.10 | **Example of HTML for Iconclass headings as generated by xsl:choose shown in figure 7.9**

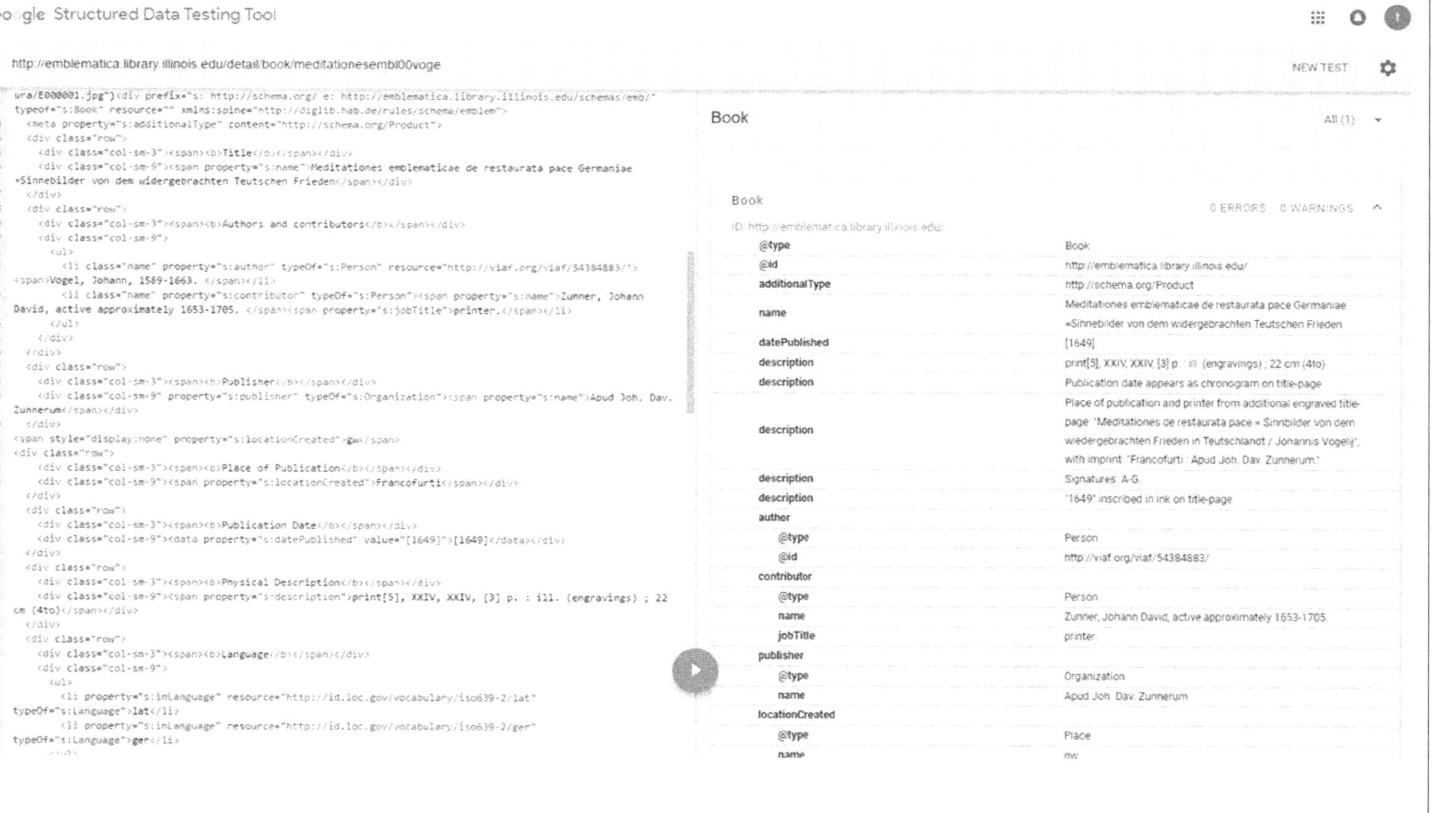

Figure 7.11 | **A book-level HTML page in Google's Structured Data Testing Tool**

(https://search.google.com/structured-data/testing-tool). As can be seen, the RDFa attributes embedded in the HTML document generated by the XSLT are extracted by Google into RDF statements (right pane) as expected. What is not entirely clear is which of these RDF statements are then used by Google when building its web search engine index. In theory, the inclusion of RDFa in HTML descriptions of emblem resources should enhance digitized emblem discoverability and better link these resources with other related resources.

CONCLUSION

Transforming or creating library data as linked data is at the center of an ongoing discussion in the library domain. There are multiple ways to create and publish library data as linked data. Various sets of RDF-friendly semantics have been proposed. The Library of Congress is developing BibFrame (https://www.loc.gov/bibframe/), a new RDF-based data model focused on bibliographic description and resource and data management. Meanwhile, OCLC has been transforming its vast store of catalog records to RDF and linked data using schema.org semantics (www.oclc.org/research/themes/data-science/linkeddata.html) and focusing on resource discoverability. The methods outlined in this chapter align with how OCLC has been experimenting with linked data, that is, using the same ontology, schema.org. The same methods, though, can be used to transform XML metadata into BibFrame. Metadata in XML can easily be transformed into various serializations of RDF, including but not limited to RDFa, using XSLT. In this way, XSLT can facilitate the use of, discovery of, and access to library data on the Web.

As alluded to above, appendixes A through C comprise a complete, stand-alone illustration of the use case described in this chapter. Appendix A, "Sample SPINE Metadata Record for an Emblem Book," provides the XML describing an emblem book and one emblem (other emblems were deleted for the sake of brevity). Appendix B is the XSLT for creating book-level HTML+RDFa. When applied to the XML of appendix A, an HTML document (with RDFa embedded) describing the emblem book results. Similarly, appendix C is the XSLT for creating emblem-level HTML+RDFa. When applied to the XML of appendix A, an HTML document (with RDFa embedded) describing the emblem on its own results. Note that the Google Structured Data Testing Tool is not the only way to see the RDF statements embedded using RDFa in the book-level and emblem-level result documents. The World Wide Web Consortium provides a different online tool, the RDFa 1.1 distiller and parser (https://www.w3.org/2012/pyRdfa/Overview.html), which also extracts and displays the RDF statements contained in an HTML+RDFa document.

An additional XSLT illustrating the transformation of rows in a spreadsheet saved as XML into JavaScript Object Notation for Linked Data (JSON-LD) is available from one of the author's GitHub repository (https://github.com/tcole3/XSLT/).

Notes

1. Timothy W. Cole, Myung-Ja K. Han, William Fletcher Weathers, and Eric Joyner, "Library MARC Records into Linked Open Data: Challenges and Opportunities," *Journal of Library Metadata* 13, no. 2–3 (2013): 163–96.
2. Timothy W. Cole, Myung-Ja K. Han, Maria Janina Sarol, Monika Biel, and David Maus, "Using Linked Open Data to Enhance the Discoverability, Functionality & Impact of Emblematica Online," *Library Hi Tech* 35, no. 1 (2017): 159–78.
3. Stephen Rawles, "A Spine of Information Headings for Emblem-Related Electronic Resources," in *Digital Collections and the Management of Knowledge: Renaissance Emblem Literature as a Case Study for the Digitization of Rare Texts and Images*, ed. M. Wade (Salzburg, 2004), 19–28.
4. R. Heery and M. Patel, "Application Profiles: Mixing and Matching Metadata Schemas," *Ariadne* 25 (September 24, 2000), www.ariadne.ac.uk/issue25/app-profiles/intro.html.

AN INTRODUCTION TO XQUERY FOR LIBRARY METADATA INCLUDING USE CASES

Catalogers and metadata librarians' work is transitioning from describing resources one at a time to working on batches of records that represent large groups of resources. Using programming for library metadata work has become attractive for accomplishing the tasks of analyzing, updating, and manipulating metadata. XQuery is a functional, declarative programming language that became a W3C recommendation in early 2007. It is designed to query, reorganize, and transform XML data. While often thought of as just a query language—SQL for XML—it is capable of doing a lot more and is actually a general-purpose programming language for working with XML.

In this chapter, real-world examples illustrate XQuery's use in one digital library setting. After this overview of XQuery's potential, chapter 9 will begin with the basics of the XQuery language.

WHY XQUERY FOR METADATA WORK?

Partially because it is an older standard, XSLT has been the favored programming language used to transform and crosswalk library metadata. However,

XQuery can do much the same thing as XSLT, with the added power of being able to query data as well as transform it. XQuery can be used to query, analyze, manipulate, and construct library metadata. So, why should a cataloger or metadata librarian consider using XQuery rather than another programming/scripting language?

- XQuery has a concise syntax, and so is faster to write than XSLT.
- XQuery is easy to pick up, and is readable for simple metadata tasks.
- XQuery is specifically designed to query and manipulate XML, one of the most common data structures currently in use for library metadata.
- XQuery is good for working with and analyzing large datasets. It is useful for navigating and isolating pieces of data.
- XQuery helps the metadata librarian think about library metadata as data, not text, since it was developed by the database community.
- XQuery 3.1 has added support for working with and returning results as JSON, a data structure used for linked data, for example, JSON-LD.

USE CASES FOR CATALOGING AND METADATA WORK

Here are a list of generic uses for XQuery with cataloging and metadata:

- Analyze and evaluate large datasets
- Metadata remediation: correct errors and clean up problematic metadata
- Repurpose and combine disparate sources of metadata (generally matching on identifiers)
- Perform global changes on name and subject string values
- Enhance and add value to metadata by inserting new elements or attributes
- Crosswalk metadata from one schema to another
- Generate new metadata XML documents programmatically
- Create a CSV file to import metadata into an Excel spreadsheet
- Query XML content and serialize output as JSON

CASE STUDY

USING XQUERY IN A LIBRARY METADATA SETTING

In this section, the Princeton Theological Seminary Library's digital projects will illustrate how XQuery can be practically used for library metadata work. The intention of this section is not to instruct the beginner, but merely to show the language's potential. XQuery has been used to correct, enhance, and create metadata using METS, Dublin Core, MARCXML, EAD, MODS, TEI, CopyrightMD, and a local schema. The Princeton Seminary Library's digital library platform, MarkLogic Server, is a proprietary NoSQL database, and all our metadata and some of our digital content is encoded in XML. MarkLogic has been expanding its database to include semantics (RDF triple stores), and the latest version includes support for JavaScript and JSON. We use XQuery for writing web applications as well as any other type of interaction with the underlying data. XQuery, XSLT, and regular expressions are our primary tools for working with metadata programmatically.

WORKING WITH LIBRARY METADATA PROGRAMMATICALLY

The library's metadata workflow for almost all digital projects follows a basic "rule"—do as much as you can with programming first and then follow with editing by hand as needed. This is the opposite of traditional library cataloging where each item is cataloged by hand one at a time. XQuery facilitates this computational approach to metadata. Part of the XQuery language is XPath 2.0. XPath is a language designed to navigate through the XML documents so that you can work through the hierarchical structure of these documents to find precisely what you are looking for. Also, XQuery is a functional programming language and lends itself to writing functions to solve discrete tasks. If you are not a programmer, you can start small with XQuery by writing queries to solve simple, everyday metadata tasks: searching and evaluating XML elements and fragments of metadata, counting items, and creating lists and reports. Once you get your metadata into an XML format, which is relatively easy to do, you can start with the first step: analyze the data.

QUERYING/ANALYZING DATASETS

The basic building block of XQuery is the FLWOR expression (FLWOR stands for: "for, let, where, order by, return"). So, I will usually start by writing simple FLWOR expressions to query the underlying data elements in isolation—identifiers, titles, names, dates, and so on. What am I dealing with? How irregular is the metadata? Are there any outliers? Understanding the metadata schema you are dealing with (including best practices) and getting a good overall sense of your dataset are key first steps to working with metadata programmatically.

PARSING METADATA VALUES

Metadata, especially from nonlibrary sources, can sometimes be irregular and inconsistent and needs some normalization and remediation work to get it into shape.

Figure 8.1 illustrates this using a METS document. In this example the dataset had 581 names for correspondence from an archival collection with 38 name fields containing multiple names, with the Dutch word "aan" separating the two names. This query limits on this pattern, builds new element nodes in our local sort namespace, and inserts these new nodes after the original one with

```
xquery version "1.0-ml";

(: Query creator elements to locate the ones containing multiple names :)

declare namespace mets = "http://www.loc.gov/METS/";
declare namespace dc = "http://purl.org/dc/elements/1.1/";
declare namespace sort = "http://digital.library.ptsem.edu/sort";

for $dmdSec in fn:doc("/METS/Kuyper118.xml")/mets:mets/mets:dmdSec/
mets:mdWrap/mets:xmlData
let $sortCreator := $dmdSec/sort:creator
let $names := fn:tokenize($sortCreator, "\saan\s")
for $name in $names
let $newNode := <sort:creator xmlns:sort="http://digital.library.
ptsem.edu/sort">{ fn:normalize-space($name) }</sort:creator>
where fn:matches($sortCreator, "\saan\s", "i")
order by $name
return xdmp:node-insert-after($sortCreator, $newNode)
```

Figure 8.1 | **A simple example of Query code**

multiple names. The end result is two `<sort:creator>` element nodes that will be used for an author browse feature in the digital library's user interface.

This example illustrates one of the strengths of a functional programming language—it is concise. You don't need a lot of XQuery code to modify metadata in a simple, efficient manner. (The next step in this editing process required another simple query to be written that deleted the original `<sort:creator>` element nodes that contained the multiple names.[1])

MANIPULATING/REPURPOSING METADATA

Three of the standard XQuery functions: `matches()`, `replace()`, and `tokenize()`, allow for the use of regular expressions and are powerful ways to match and modify string values.

The example shown in figure 8.2 illustrates this. The original source of this metadata was a database from another department at our institution that

```
(:
 : Returns a <series> element containing the series title from the
500 field of the MARC record (there may be more than one series for an
individual AV item).
 :)
declare function av:get-av-series-from-note($marc as element(m:record)?)
as element(ia:series)*
{
  let $seriesTitle := $marc/m:datafield[@tag = ("410", "440", "490")][1]
  let $_500s := $marc/m:datafield[@tag = "500"]
  for $_500 in $_500s
  where fn:not($seriesTitle)
  and fn:matches($_500, "lectures?(\s|$)", "i") (: Avoids "lectureship" :)
            or fn:matches($_500, "symposium", "i")
            or fn:matches($_500, "conference", "i")
            or fn:matches($_500, "seminar(\s|$)", "i") (: Avoids
"Seminary" :)
            or fn:matches($_500, "I\.?O\.?T\.?", "i")
            or fn:matches($_500, "institute", "i")
            or fn:matches($_500, "series(\s|$)", "i")
            or fn:matches($_500, "forum", "i"))
  return <series xmlns="http://digital.library.ptsem.edu/ia">{
fn:normalize-space($_500) }</series>
};
```

Figure 8.2 | **Query illustrating the use of regular expressions with the `matches()` function**

had been converted to MARC records (using MarcEdit) and loaded into our library catalog over ten years ago. I used Ex Libris Voyager's RESTful APIs to extract the MARC as MARCXML. In this example, we wanted to locate possible lecture series titles that were mapped to a 500 note field during the earlier data migration. The `matches()` function looks for values we identified during the analysis phase.

BUILDING URLS AND WORKING WITH APIS

As datasets become freely available, working with APIs is becoming more important for capturing metadata to work with and reuse. We have used several APIs (Internet Archive, Ex Libris Voyager, and OCLC) to capture metadata to reuse for digital projects. Figure 8.3 is an example of a query that uses a Voyager RESTful API to query our library catalog's database for MARC records that correspond to EAD finding aids. I enhanced the subject headings for these finding aids in the Voyager cataloging module and then extracted them from Voyager and embedded the subject headings into the EAD finding aid with another query.

```
xquery version "1.0-ml";

declare namespace html = "http://www.w3.org/1999/xhtml";
declare namespace zs = "http://www.loc.gov/zing/srw/";
declare namespace m = "http://www.loc.gov/MARC21/slim";
declare namespace ead = "urn:isbn:1-931666-22-9";

for $doc in xdmp:directory("/EAD/")
let $title := $doc/ead:ead/ead:eadheader/ead:filedesc/ead:titlestmt/
ead:titleproper
let $titleString := fn:normalize-space(fn:substring($title, 5))
let $noPunctuationTitle := fn:replace($titleString, "\p{P}", "")
let $queryTitle := fn:string-join(fn:subsequence(fn:tokenize($no
PunctuationTitle, " "), 1, 5), "+")
let $queries := fn:concat('http://catalog.ptsem.edu:7095/voyager?
version=1.1&amp;maximumRecords=1000&amp;recordSchema=marcxml&amp;
operation=searchRetrieve&amp;query=', '"', $queryTitle, '"')
for $query at $count in $queries
let $http := xdmp:http-get($query)
return fn:normalize-space($title)
```

Figure 8.3 | **Query that uses Ex Libris Voyager RESTful API to extract MARC records**

```
xquery version "1.0-ml";

(: This query adds the @integer attribute to the <number> element :)

declare namespace ia = "http://digital.library.ptsem.edu/ia";
declare namespace m = "http://www.loc.gov/MARC21/slim";

let $docs := xdmp:directory("/ia-xml/d/", "infinity")
for $doc in $docs
let $number := $doc/ia:doc/ia:metadata/ia:volumeInfo/ia:number
let $numValue := fn:replace($number, "^(\d+)(\-|\s*).*$", "$1")
where $number
      and $numValue castable as xs:integer
      and fn:not($number/@integer)
return (xdmp:set-request-time-limit(3600), xdmp:node-insert-
child($number, attribute integer { $numValue }))
```

Figure 8.4 | **Query that illustrates working with numbers**

WORKING WITH NUMBERS

While it is much more common to use XQuery for string manipulation for library metadata, there are times when you have to work with numbers. This next example shown in figure 8.4 adds a number attribute where the value is extracted from a string using regular expressions and is tested to see if it is an integer. The functions with the xdmp namespace prefix are MarkLogic vendor-defined functions that allow changes to the data. Alternatively, in an open-source environment such as BaseX, XQuery Update Facility expressions are used to change or modify data.

COUNTING AND WORKING WITH SEQUENCES

As you test and evaluate the correctness of your code, it is often necessary to count your results before permanently making changes to the data. It also helps to count how many items you are dealing with or how many things need to be changed. This next example illustrates the `count()` function and is also a good example of the importance of working with sequences; in fact, when I was first learning XQuery, I was advised that "in XQuery everything is a sequence." The example in figure 8.5 is a main module consisting of the two user-defined functions (which are in the local namespace) `local:get-collection-counts()` and `local:count-collection-names()`.

```
xquery version "1.0-ml";

declare namespace ia = "http://digital.library.ptsem.edu/ia";
declare namespace m = "http://www.loc.gov/MARC21/slim";

(: Returns a list of collection names taken from MARC 730. :)
declare function local:get-collection-names()
as xs:string*
{
  for $doc in fn:collection()[fn:position() = (1 to 1000)] (: TODO:
run over entire database :)
  let $marc := $doc/ia:doc/ia:metadata/ia:marc/m:record
  let $collections := $marc/m:datafield[@tag = "730"][@ind2 = " "]
  for $collection in $collections
  let $collectionString := fn:normalize-space($collection)
  let $contributor := $doc/ia:doc/ia:metadata/ia:contributor
  where fn:not(fn:matches($collectionString, "Benson|Torrance")) (:
filter out Benson and Torrance items :)
    and fn:matches($collectionString, "collection|library", "i") (:
test for keywords found in PTS collection names to filter out other
values :)
    and fn:contains($contributor, "Princeton Theological Seminary")
(: only look at PTS items :)
  order by $collectionString
  (: remove final period from collection names :)
  return fn:replace($collectionString, "\.$", "")
};

(: For each collection name, returns the number of occurrences in the
database :)
declare function local:get-collection-counts()
as xs:string*
{
  let $collection-titles := local:get-collection-names()
  for $collection in fn:distinct-values($collection-titles)
  (: fn:index-of() returns a sequence listing the numerical position
of each appearance of the unique collection name ($collection) in the
full list of collection titles ($collection-titles). fn:count() counts
each item in the sequence. :)
  let $count := fn:count(fn:index-of($collection-titles, $collection))
  order by $count descending
  return fn:concat($count, " ", $collection)
};

local:get-collection-counts()
```

Figure 8.5 | **Query that illustrates two user-defined functions that work with sequences**

WORKING WITH IDENTIFIERS/URIS

Working with identifiers and URIs is an important part of manipulating metadata with programming because unique identifiers are the best way to match data coming from various sources. The next example (figure 8.6) illustrates this point. In this case, I had two sources of MARCXML metadata for audio recordings—the library catalog and data from a spreadsheet that I mapped to MARC using MarcEdit. I had to locate items from the spreadsheet that were not in the library catalog. This main module finds the unique identifiers that were not in the library catalog and imports another module that contains the functions needed to create new XML documents for our Theological Commons application.

MODIFYING COMPLEX DOCUMENTS

METS documents can be very lengthy and complex. It is not uncommon to only want to modify one section of a METS document. This can be done with XQuery by using XPath to navigate to the part of the METS document that you want to change. In the example shown in figure 8.7, we added a `TYPE` attribute to identify page images of the digital object that are blank. This attribute value is needed for a feature in the user interface that allows the user to hide or show the blank pages in a manuscript collection. It is also a good example of the human/machine distribution of labor because the blank page images had to be identified by human review, and a list of file names needed to be created for this query to work.

REPURPOSING/CONSTRUCTING/CROSSWALKING METADATA WITH LIBRARY MODULES

In XQuery, code is organized as main modules or library modules. For crosswalking metadata, for example, MARCXML to MODS, I will write a library module with a separate function for each element for the final metadata output. Usually I will write two more functions: one to build the new XML document, and finally one to add the new XML document to the database. Organizing the mapping/crosswalk functions by metadata element (or single tasks) simplifies the code and makes it more readable and easier to troubleshoot when you need

```
xquery version "1.0-ml";

(: Query to create theocom XML documents from the Ed. Media audio
spreadsheet :)

import module namespace av = "http://digital.library.ptsem.edu/ia/av-
marc" at "Apps/theocom-chris/admin/av-marc.xqy";
declare namespace m = "http://www.loc.gov/MARC21/slim";

declare function local:find-unique-ids() as xs:string*
{  let $newMARCXMLs :=
     for $uri in cts:uris("/new-marcxml/")
     let $newID := fn:substring(fn:replace(fn:substring-after($uri, "/
new-marcxml/"), ".xml", ""), 1, 4)
     return $newID

  let $oldMARCXMLs :=
    for $uri in cts:uris("/MARCXML/")
    let $id := fn:replace(fn:substring-after($uri, "/MARCXML/"),
".xml", "")
    let $tokenizedIDs := fn:tokenize($id, "--") (: Tokenize id numbers
that are in ranges to evaluate 2nd number :)
    for $tokenizedID in $tokenizedIDs
    return fn:substring($tokenizedID, 1, 4)

(: Iterate through the new IDs and compare each ID to the sequence of
old IDs to locate ones that don't match :)
  for $newMARCXML in $newMARCXMLs
  where $newMARCXML
  order by $newMARCXML
  return
    if ($newMARCXML = $oldMARCXMLs) then
       ()
    else $newMARCXML (: Sequence of the 1st 4 digits for new ids to
add to theocom-av-prep database :)
};

for $doc in xdmp:directory("/new-marcxml/")[fn:position() = (1 to 25)]
let $marc := $doc/m:record
let $idSeq := local:find-unique-ids()
let $newID := fn:substring(fn:replace(fn:substring-after(fn:base-
uri($doc), "/new-marcxml/"), ".xml", ""), 1, 4)
let $rootNode := av:build-av-theocom-document($marc)
let $uri := fn:concat("/theocom-audio/", av:get-av-identifier($marc),
".xml")
where  $newID = $idSeq
return xdmp:document-insert($uri, $rootNode)
```

Figure 8.6 | **Query that illustrates working with identifiers**

```
xquery version "1.0-ml";

(: 9/16/11 Query for adding blank page attributes to structMap of
METS documents using a sequence of file names from blank page reports.
Modified on 3/9/12 to adjust for new div structure :)

declare namespace mets = "http://www.loc.gov/METS/";
declare namespace xlink = "http://www.w3.org/1999/xlink";

let $doc := fn:doc("/METS/Kuyper239-241.xml")
let $file-names := ("/240-0001t", "/240-0002t", "/240-0004t", "/240-
0006t", "/240-0008t", "/240-0012t")
let $images := for $file-name in $file-names
               return fn:concat("Manuscripts/thumb/Kuyper/239-241",
$file-name, ".jpg")
for $image in $images
for $file-location in $doc/mets:mets//mets:FLocat
where $image = $file-location/@xlink:href
return for $id in $file-location/parent::mets:file/@ID
       for $file-id in $doc/mets:mets/mets:structMap//mets:div/
mets:fptr where $id = $file-id/@FILEID
       return xdmp:node-insert-child($file-id/parent::mets:div,
attribute TYPE { "blank-page" })
```

Figure 8.7 | **Query that illustrates modifying one section of a METS document**

to reuse or change the code. Figure 8.8 shows one of these functions. This function, called `av:get-av-date()`, extracts the date value from MARC records that come from two different sources: the Voyager catalog and a spreadsheet. The conditions in the return clause check for a four-digit date in two different ways based on the source metadata.

The example shown in figure 8.9 illustrates a function to build a complete new XML document. The return clause in this function builds the new document. While you cannot see the details of all the functions called here, this example illustrates how each one does a separate task to create the new document. A lot is happening with each function call. Besides building new elements, a function from another module uses OCLC's WorldCat Search API to retrieve an appropriate call number when the MARC record lacks one. Furthermore, the Library of Congress call number is used by another module to classify the item and automatically create a subject facet for the user interface. So using XQuery functions is a very clean, efficient way to transform and repurpose metadata when you have several complex steps to go through.

```
(: This function extracts the date value for the original recording
from the MARC record. It uses the character position for the first
or second 4-digit date from the 008 fixed field. For the date types
coded "p", "r" or "t" the second date is the date of the original
recording. :)

declare function av:get-av-date($marc as node()*)
as xs:string?
{
 let $dateType := fn:substring($marc/m:controlfield[@tag = "008"], 7, 1)
  let $date1 := fn:substring($marc/m:controlfield[@tag = "008"], 8, 4)
  let $date2 := fn:substring($marc/m:controlfield[@tag = "008"], 12, 4)
  let $_518 := $marc/m:datafield[@tag = "518"]
  return
    (: Condition added for metadata from Ed. Media audio spreadsheet
to get date from 518 field, rather than 008 fixed field. :)
    if ($dateType = "s" and $date1 = "9999" and fn:matches($_518, "\
d+")) then
            fn:normalize-space(fn:tokenize($_518, "/")[fn:position()
= fn:last()])
    else if ($dateType = "s" and $date1 castable as xs:gYear) then
                  $date1
         else if ($dateType = ("p", "r", "t") and $date2 castable as
xs:gYear) then
                       $date2
              else ()
};
```

Figure 8.8 | **Example of a user-defined function from a library module**

```
(: This is the main function of the module. It constructs the theocom
document for the Theological Commons application including the full
MARC record. For the title element, the regular expression removes
most ending punctuation except dash, bracket, parenthesis, quote or
connector. The contributor element has the Theological Commons default
value for Princeton Seminary. :)

declarefunctionav:build-av-theocom-document($marcaselement(m:record)?)
as element(ia:doc)
{
  let $name := marc:get-name($marc)
  let $date := av:get-av-date($marc)
  let $call-num := marc:get-call-number($marc)
  return
    <doc xmlns="http://digital.library.ptsem.edu/ia">
      <metadata>
        { av:get-av-identifier($marc) }
        { if ($name) then <name>{ $name }</name> else () }
        <title>
          { fn:normalize-space(fn:replace(av:create-brief-av-title
($marc),"(\s*\p{Po}+\s*)$", "")) }
        </title>
        <sortTitle first-letter="{ marc:create-first-letter($marc) }">
          { av:build-sort-av-title($marc) }
        </sortTitle>
        { marc:get-uniform-title($marc) }
        { marc:get-edition($marc) }
           { av:get-duration($marc) }
           { av:get-recording-date($marc) }
        { av:get-av-series($marc) }
           { av:get-av-series-from-note($marc) }
        { if (fn:empty($date)) then () else <date>{ $date }</date> }
        { marc:get-language($marc) }
        { av:get-av-format($marc) }
        { av:get-av-notes($marc) }
        { $call-num }
        <class>{ class:map-class(normalize-space($call-num)) }</class>
        { av:get-av-genre($marc) }
        { av:revise-av-topics($marc) }
      <contributor>Princeton Theological Seminary Library</contributor>
        <marc>{ $marc }</marc>
      </metadata>
    </doc>
};
```

'igure 8.9 | **Example of a user-defined function that creates a new XML document**

Note

1. If you are a stickler for details, you may have noticed that the Dutch word "aan" means "to" and that the second name is the recipient of the letter, not the author. This is a good example of the iterative development when repurposing metadata that requires a conversation with one of our programmers about including a new element, `<sort:contributor>`, or not.

XQUERY BASICS

This chapter will provide a brief overview of some of the most important parts of the XQuery language. First, however, here is a list of some basic vocabulary terms that are commonly used in most programming languages.[1]

SOME BASIC PROGRAMMING CONCEPTS AND VOCABULARY

Expression: A statement that evaluates to some value.

Variable: A symbolic name for a piece of data. In XQuery, a variable is bound to a particular value and that value does not change.

Function: A "self-contained" module of code that accomplishes a specific task. Functions "take in" data, process it, and "return" a result.

Literals: A constant value, or a value that is written exactly as it's meant to be interpreted. It can be a string literal or a numeric literal.

Tuple: An ordered list of elements, that is, a sequence of elements. This sequence is referred to as "tuple stream" and is an important concept for XQuery FLWOR expression.

Operands and Operators: Expressions are made up of operands and operators. Operand is the data to be manipulated or operated on. Operator is a symbol that represents a specific action, for example, "+" for addition.

Parameters: A parameter is a variable used in a function definition.

Arguments: An argument is the data passed into a function's parameters.

API: An abbreviation for application programming interfaces. They are procedures or protocols that enable one computer program to talk to another.

XQUERY BASICS: STRUCTURE

- Anatomy of an XQuery file
- Main module (executable code)
- Library module (stored code, not executable)
- Main module consists of a prolog and a body
    - Prolog contains declarations
    - Body contains a single expression
- For a good overview of module organization, see *XQuery Style Conventions,* 2006, http://xqdoc.org/xquery-style.pdf.

XQUERY MAIN MODULE

XQuery and XPath Data Model (XDM)

It is possible to start writing queries without a deep understanding of the XQuery data model, but as one's skills develop, the data model becomes important for writing good XQuery code. See figure 9.1. This is an outline of the XQuery data model. The following terms[2] will be used in later chapters where functions are discussed.

Node: An XML construct

Atomic value: A simple data value without markup

Item: Generic term for either node or atomic value

```
xquery version "1.0-ml";

import module namespace rights = "http://digital.library.ptsem.edu/
kuyper-dl/admin/rights-metadata" at "/rights-metadata.xqy";

declare namespace mets = "http://www.loc.gov/METS/";
declare namespace dc = "http://purl.org/dc/elements/1.1/";
declare namespace c = "http://www.cdlib.org/inside/diglib/copyrightMD";

let $docs := xdmp:directory("/METS/")
for $dmdSec in $docs/mets:mets/mets:dmdSec
let $format := $dmdSec/mets:mdWrap/mets:xmlData/dc:type
let $copyMeta := $dmdSec/mets:mdWrap/mets:xmlData/c:copyright
where $format = "Book" and fn:not($copyMeta)
return rights:build-metadata-for-books($dmdSec)
```

Figure 9.1 | **Illustration of an XQuery main module that imports a library module**

Sequence: An ordered list of zero, one, or more items

Seven node kinds:

1. Document
2. Element
3. Attribute
4. Text
5. Comment
6. Namespace
7. Processing instruction

XML Constructors

Repurposing metadata from one data structure to another has become an essential skill for working with the wide variety of library and nonlibrary data that a cataloger or metadata librarian is expected to manage. Creating new XML is a key feature of XQuery. There are two ways to create new XML elements and attributes: the direct element constructor and the computed constructor. The direct element constructor is more common, but the computed constructor is often used when the name of an element or attribute is not known and is generated dynamically. Figures 9.2 and 9.3 provide examples of both types of XML constructors.

```
for $doc in xdmp:directory("/EAD/")
let $name := fn:string($doc/ead/archdesc/did/origination/persname)
order by $name ascending
return
  <controlaccess>
    <persname encodinganalog="100" role="creator" source="lcnaf" >
      { $name }
    </persname>
  </controlaccess>
```

Figure 9.2 | **A direct element constructor**

```
xdmp:node-insert-child($number, attribute integer { $numValue })

xdmp:node-replace($name/text(), text { "Società di studi valdesi" })
```

Figure 9.3 | **Two computed constructors using MarkLogic update functions**

Path Expressions

The XPath language was introduced in chapter 5. XPath 2.0 is an important part, a subset, of the XQuery programming language. The importance of understanding XPath in order to work successfully with XQuery cannot be overstated. It is essential for becoming a good XQuery developer.

FLWOR Expressions

As mentioned in chapter 8, the most important expression of the XQuery language is the FLWOR (pronounced "flower") expression. FLWOR expressions must have at least one for or let clause and a return clause. See figure 9.4. The where clause must come before the order by clause, and both are optional.

For clause: This clause iterates through each item in a sequence.

Let clause: This clause binds a variable to a value.

Where clause: This clause filters the results to exclude items based on a given condition.

Order by clause: This clause sorts the results.

Return clause: This clause specifies the results.

```
xquery version "1.0-ml";
(: 2/4/15 Query to change names to LCNAF form :)
declare namespace ia = "http://digital.library.ptsem.edu/ia";
for $meta in collection()//ia:doc/ia:metadata
let $names := $meta/ia:name
for $name in $names
where $name = "McMickel, Marvin A."
return xdmp:node-replace($name/text(), text{ "McMickle, Marvin Andrew"}
```

Figure 9.4 | **A FLWOR expression**

Joins

The concept of a join comes from the SQL query language. In XQuery, the join is very helpful to join data from multiple sources.[3] In figure 9.5, the two where clauses join data from the incoming file ids and file names/ids in two sections of a METS document, the file section and the structural map.

```
let $doc := doc("/METS/Kuyper239-241.xml")
let $file-names := ("/240-0001t", "/240-0002t", "/240-0004t", "/240-
0006t", "/240-0008t", "/240-0012t")
let $images := for $file-name in $file-names
               return concat("Manuscripts/thumb/Kuyper/239-241", $file-
name, ".jpg")
for $image in $images
for $file-location in $doc/mets:mets//mets:FLocat
where $image = $file-location/@xlink:href
return for $id in $file-location/parent::mets:file/@ID
       for $file-id in
  $doc/mets:mets/mets:structMap//mets:div/mets:fptr
       where $id = $file-id/@FILEID
       return xdmp:node-insert-child($file-id/parent::mets:div,
attribute TYPE { "blank-page" })
```

Figure 9.5 | **An example of two joins that uses the where clauses**

Conditional Expressions (if-then-else)

Testing for conditions in the metadata is a common aspect of coding work with metadata, looking for certain values, or treating problems in a specific way. In figure 9.6, the if-then-else expression locates audio and video recordings in MARCXML records and assigns a format facet value to each.

```
(: Returns a <format> element indicating the AV format of the item. The
general material designation (subfield h) contains the AV format. :)

declare function av:get-av-format($marc as element(m:record)?)as
element(ia:format)
{
  let $avFormat := $marc/m:datafield[@tag = "245"]/m:subfield[@code = "h"]
  let $value :=
    if (matches($avFormat, "videorecording", "i")) then

      "Video"
    else if (matches($avFormat, "sound recording","i")) then

         "Audio"
       else ()
  return <format xmlns="http://digital.library.ptsem.edu/ia">{ $value
}</format>
};

(: This function extracts date value for the original recording from
the MARC record. It uses the character position for the first or second
4-digit date from the 008 fixed field. For the date types coded "p", "r"
or "t" the second date is the date of the orignial recording. :)
declare function av:get-av-date($marc as node()*)
as xs:string?
{
  let $dateType := substring($marc/m:controlfield[@tag = "008"], 7, 1)
  let $date1 := substring($marc/m:controlfield[@tag = "008"], 8, 4)
  let $date2 := substring($marc/m:controlfield[@tag = "008"], 12, 4)
  let $_518 := $marc/m:datafield[@tag = "518"]
  return
    (: Condition added for metadata from Ed. Media audio spreadsheet
to get date from 518 field, rather than 008 fixed field. :)
    if ($dateType = "s" and $date1 = "9999" and matches($_518, "\d+"))
then
           normalize-space(fn:tokenize($_518, "/")[position() =
last()])
    else if ($dateType = "s" and $date1 castable as xs:gYear) then
                $date1
         else if ($dateType = ("p", "r", "t") and $date2 castable as
xs:gYear) then
                     $date2
              else ()
};
```

Figure 9.6 | **Conditional expressions in the return clause**

```
declare function av:get-av-series-from-note($marc as
element(m:record)?)
as element(ia:series)*
{
  let $seriesTitle := $marc/m:datafield[@tag = ("410", "440", "490")][1]
  let $_500s := $marc/m:datafield[@tag = "500"]
  for $_500 in $_500s
  where not($seriesTitle)
    and (matches($_500, "lectures?(\s|$)", "i") (: Avoids "lectureship" :)
      or matches($_500, "symposium", "i")
      or matches($_500, "conference", "i")
      or matches($_500, "seminar(\s|$)", "i") (: Avoids "Seminary" :)
      or matches($_500, "I\.?O\.?T\.?", "i")
      or matches($_500, "institute", "i")
      or matches($_500, "series(\s|$)", "i")
      or matches($_500, "forum", "i"))
  return <series xmlns="http://digital.library.ptsem.edu/ia">{
normalize-space($_500) }</series>
};
```

Figure 9.7 | **Logical expressions (and, or) in the where clause**

Logical Expressions (and/or)

Most librarians are familiar with the Boolean operators `and` and `or`. Figure 9.7 uses these operators to test for the Boolean values `true` and `false`. Where the conditions are true, a new series element is created for a local metadata schema. This is an example of repurposing metadata before any human review happens. It also illustrates a user-defined function. Functions in XQuery are the subject of the next chapter.

Notes

1. Some of the programming language definitions are from www.cs.utah.edu/~germain/PPS/Topics/.
2. These XQuery Data Model term definitions are from Priscilla Walmsley, *XQuery: Search across a Variety of XML Data,* 2nd edition (Sebastopol, CA: O'Reilly Media, 2016), 21–23.
3. Walmsley, *XQuery,* 95.

XQUERY FUNCTIONS INCLUDING REGULAR EXPRESSIONS

Functions are an important part of the XQuery programming language. "Almost 200 functions are built into XQuery, covering a broad range of functionality. Functions can be used to manipulate strings and dates, perform mathematical calculations, combine sequences of elements, and perform many other useful jobs. You can also define your own functions, either in the query itself, or in an external library."[1]

Next we will take a look at some of the XQuery built-in functions that are particularly useful with cataloging and metadata work. Then we will consider some user-defined functions, including instructions on how to write your own user-defined functions.

FUNCTIONS FOR WORKING WITH STRINGS

So much of cataloging and metadata content is textual string values. Some of the most practical XQuery functions for working with strings are:

- compare()
- concat()
- contains()
- ends-with()

- lower-case()
- matches()
- normalize-space()
- replace()
- starts-with()
- string-join()
- substring()
- substring-after()
- substring-before()
- tokenize()

In figure 10.1, we are querying a dataset of MARCXML records that were downloaded from a library catalog. The query looks for three pieces of information: bibliographic record id number, call number, and title. It then builds a CSV file that will be imported into Excel. One of the functions shown in the query is `contains()`, since we are looking for a title that contains the word "Yoruba." The where clause limits to only those MARCXML records which have that word in the title. Another function is `concat()`, which is used to create the string of metadata values needed for the CSV file.

Some other important functions when working with string values in metadata are:

The function `normalize-space()` should always be used with strings to remove whitespace in a string. For example, `normalize- space(doc/metadata/title)` will remove

```
declare namespace m = "http://www.loc.gov/MARC21/slim";

let $headers := "BIB ID,CALL NO.,TITLE"

let $metadata:=
  for $records in collection()
  let $bib-id := normalize-space($records/m:record/m:controlfield[@tag
= "001"])
  let $call-nums := $records/m:record/m:datafield[@tag = ("050", "055",
"090", "099")][1]
  let $title := $records/m:record/m:datafield[@tag = "245"]/(* except
m:subfield[@code = [1]
  where contains($title, "Yoruba")
  order by $bib-id
  return concat($bib-id, ',', $call-nums, '"', $title, '"')

return ($headers, $metadata)
```

Figure 10.1 | **Query that illustrates working with strings**

all leading and trailing spaces, collapse consecutive spaces into a single space, and replace carriage return, line feed, and tab with a single space. It is recommended to use this function on all string data.

The function `translate()` will replace characters in a string with other characters. So, to build a new attribute called "`xsi:schemaLocation`" we can use this function to change the value from "Z" to "R": `attribute xsi:schemaLocation { translate($schemaLoc, "Z", "R") })`

There is no limit to how many functions can be nested. So, you can have something like this: `replace(substring-after($doc, "/theocom-xml/"), ".xml", "")`. In this instance the `substring-after()` function is called as the first argument of the `replace()` function.

Sometimes the beginning or the end of a string will be enough to identify the value (or in XML parlance, the element node content) that you need to extract. Here is a common example from cataloging. A MARCXML record may contain several 035 fields, but you only want the ones containing an OCLC control number. This is an example for locating these: `starts-with (normalize-space($controlNum), "(OCoLC)")`, because all the OCLC control numbers begin with "(OCoLC)."

Similarly, you may want to exclude initial articles from title values to create a title field to sort on. The `substring()` function will work in this case. For example, if all the titles in the dataset started with the initial article "The", the substring function can extract everything after the article and one space: `substring($title, 5)`. The function will extract the title starting at the fifth character and capture the rest of the title string. While this may seem like an artificial example, it comes from a real use case of EAD finding aids which consistently had titles that started with the initial article "The."

Another helpful function is `string-join()`, which concatenates a sequence of strings together with an optional separator. For example, `string -join($seq, " ")` takes a sequence of URIs and joins them together with a space as the separator. Or you may want to join some, but not all, of a MARCXML field. In this real case, we only wanted subfield `$a` and subfield `$p` of the uniform title:

```
string-join($marc/m:datafield[@tag = ("130",
"240")]/m:subfield[@code = ("a", "p")], " ").
```

FUNCTIONS THAT USE REGULAR EXPRESSIONS

Regular expressions, also called regexes, are special characters that are used for pattern matching of strings. There are four XQuery functions that allow the use of regular expressions: `matches()`, `replace()`, `tokenize()`, and `analyze-string()`. Since regular expression syntax and rules are beyond the scope of this book, I refer the reader to Priscilla Walmsley's second edition of *XQuery: Search across a Variety of XML Data,* chapter 19, which provides a clear explanation of regular expressions specific to XQuery, since there are several flavors of regexes out there.[2]

A few examples are in order, because regular expressions are a very important part of working programmatically with metadata. While it can be challenging to master regular expressions, doing so is time well spent because pattern matching provides so much power to program successfully with library data.

In this example, `replace($volume, "^(\d+)(\-|\s*).*$", "$1")`, the volume number is extracted from a string of numbers to be used to create an attribute that will order volumes by number in the digital library's user interface. For this function call, all punctuation is removed from the title: `replace($titleString, "\p{P}", "")`. The `matches()` function will match a pattern provided in the second argument. So, `matches($sortTitle, "^\p{P}+\s*")` looks for the `$sortTitle` that begins with punctuation and the query then goes on to remove the punctuation, so that a sort index can be created that will sort on the first letter of each title.

FUNCTIONS FOR WORKING WITH NODES AND SEQUENCES

After strings, the other group of functions that are practical for cataloging and metadata work are those that deal with nodes and sequences. Here are some that are very helpful:

- count()
- data()
- deep-equal()
- distinct-values()
- empty()
- exists()
- index-of ()
- insert-before()
- last()
- position()
- remove()
- reverse()
- string()
- subsequence()

Even though the XQuery language has expanded in version 3.1 to include maps and arrays, it is helpful to think of XQuery's return value as always returning a sequence.

There may be occasions where only a part of a sequence is needed. In this example, we needed only the first five words of the `<ead:titleproper>` for a query that would use an API to search the library catalog:

```
string-join(fn:subsequence(fn:tokenize
($noPunctuationTitle, " "), 1, 5), "+").
```

There are three nested functions used, so it is a challenge to read! The title was normalized with punctuation removed and assigned to a variable named `$noPunctuationTitle`. That title was tokenized on the space and so broken into a sequence. Finally, the `subsequence()` function starts with the first item and extracts five items which are then joined together with the `string-join()` function, using the plus sign as the separator. The end result looks like this:

```
Archibald+Alexander+Hodge+Manuscript+Collection.
```

Frequently the value needs to be extracted from the XML markup for repurposing metadata. There are a couple of ways to do this with functions in XQuery: the two functions `data()` and `string()`. The `data()` function will extract the typed value, if there is one, and the `string()` function returns the string value. So, `string($record/marc:datafield[@tag="245"]/marc:subfield[@code="a"])` would extract the value of subfield a for a title value without the markup. Normally, you would assign a long XPath expression to a variable, for example, `$title`, so that when you call the function it reads `string($title)`, which is much clearer and easier to understand. Using a variable is particularly important if your query reused the XPath expression in more than one place.

Sometimes it is very important to know the position of an item within a sequence and to test for the last item. In the case `$dmdSec/child::*[position()=last()]`, the expression is looking for the last child node in part of a METS document, the dmdSec.

Two indispensable functions for cataloging and metadata work are `count()` and `distinct-values()`. As already mentioned, the return value in XQuery will always return a sequence. When you wrap your query in the `count()` function, you will get the number of items as an integer. The next example, which is a FLWOR expression, locates EAD documents lacking subject headings. The `count()` function gives a result of 6. So, we have 6 finding aids in the database that lack subject headings. See figure 10.2.

```
count(
   for $doc in collection()
   let $controlAccess := $doc/ead:ead/ead:archdesc/ead:
controlaccess[2]
   let $title := $doc/ead:ead/ead:eadheader/ead:filedesc/ead: title
stmt/ead:titleproper
   where not($controlAccess)
   return base-uri($doc)
)
```

Figure 10.2 | **Query that uses the count() function to locate EAD documents lacking subject headings**

```
distinct-values(
    let $docs := collection()
    for $did in $docs/ead:ead/ead:archdesc/ead:dsc//
ead:did
    let $uri := base-uri($did)
 where not($did/ead:unittitle)
   and not($did/ead:unitdate)
    order by $uri
    return $uri
)
```

Figure 10.3 | **Example of a query that uses the distinct-values() function**

The function `distinct-values()` returns a sequence of unique values. If you have, for example, duplicate title or author values, only one unique value for each will be returned. In figure 10.3 we are looking for `<ead:did>` elements that lack either `<ead:unitdate>` or `<ead:unittitle>` child elements. The return value is the file and its location in the database, for example, `/EAD-test/Academy of Homiletics.xml`. The `distinct-values()` function strips out all duplicates listing each file once. Similar to the `count()` function the `distinct-values()` function contains the query for its argument.

USER-DEFINED FUNCTIONS

This section has two objectives: (1) review how to write your own user-defined function, and (2) look at examples of user-defined functions.

How to Write a User-Defined Function

As a query author, you can create your own functions, which are technically called user-defined functions. This type of function can be created in a query in a main module or located in an external library, a library module.

A user-defined function must use a prefixed name; that is, be in a namespace. A built-in prefix, `local:`, is for locally declared functions in a main module. Separate library modules generally will have their own namespace and namespace prefix.

There are several parts of a function: the function declaration and its name, a body, and a parameter list (parameters are also called "arguments"). The function declaration starts with the keyword `declare function`. The inputs and output of a function define the function signature. An XQuery function signature is made up of the function name, the parameters, and the return type. The body of the function is wrapped in curly braces and ends with a semicolon. Figure 10.4 is an example of a user-defined function from a library module. This function, called `aimeta:get-title()`, illustrates the different parts of the function. The input type is a `node()` and the output is a new element, `<mods:titleInfo>`. The input documents are metadata from the Archive-It web archiving service, where each item archived has what is called "seed" metadata. We repurposed this seed metadata to generate MODS documents that are included in our digital collections federated search and in a commercial discovery layer, ProQuest Summon, in order to enhance the

```
    declare function aimeta:get-title($doc as node()*) as
element(mods:titleInfo)
    {
        let $title := $doc/doc/seed/metadata/title return
            if (matches($title, "^The\s")) then
                <titleInfo xmlns="http://www.loc.gov/mods/v3">
                    <nonSort>The </nonSort>
                    <title>{ normalize-space(substring($title, 5))
}</title>
                </titleInfo>
            else
                <titleInfo xmlns="http://www.loc.gov/mods/v3">
                    <title>{ normalize-space($title) }</title>
                </titleInfo>
    };
```

Figure 10.4 | **Example of a user-defined function `aimeta:get-title()`**

```
declare function local:get-collection-names() as xs:string* {
  (: Finds unique collection names other than Benson and Torrance :)
  for $doc in fn:collection()
  let $marc := $doc/ia:doc/ia:metadata/ia:marc/m:record
  let $collections := $marc/m:datafield[@tag = "730"][@ind2 = " "]
  for $collection in $collections
  let $collectionString := fn:normalize-space($collection)
  where fn:not(fn:matches($collectionString, "Benson|Torrance"))
    (: Tests for keywords found in PTS collection names to filter out
other values :)
    and fn:matches($collectionString, "collection|library", "i")
  order by $collectionString
  (: Removes final period from collection names :)
  return fn:replace($collectionString, "\.$", "")
};
```

Figure 10.5 | **Example of a user-defined function `local:get-collection-names()`**

discoverability of our web archive content. Each element of the Archive-It metadata is mapped to the MODS schema.

A second example of a user-defined function can be found in figure 10.5. This example shows what this type of function looks like when it is part of the query of a main module and is not stored in an external library. The key feature is the "local" prefix, which is the default prefix for user-defined functions. There are no parameters (which are optional), but there is a return type following the keyword `as`, specifying that the result has to be a sequence of zero, one, or many strings. This function returns a list of collection names taken from the MARCXML 730 field, a field used locally for collection headings.

Notes

1. Priscilla Walmsley, *XQuery: Search across a Variety of XML Data*, 2nd edition (Sebastopol, CA: O'Reilly Media, 2016), 11.
2. Walmsley, *XQuery*, 299–313.

METADATA WORKFLOW USING XQUERY

Creating HathiTrust Submission Files for Monograph and Serials Print Holdings

This chapter will provide a practical example of a metadata workflow that uses the XQuery language. The power of XQuery to query and isolate pieces of data will be illustrated.

In 2016, our library's administration was considering HathiTrust membership. The first requirement was to submit detailed data about our print holdings, so we could obtain from HathiTrust what the financial cost of our membership would be. The goal of this project was to prepare three tab-separated values (TSV) files of our library's print holdings. There were basically two broad steps in the process to prepare the data for HathiTrust. First, export bibliographic and holdings records (including item data) in the form of MARCXML records from our Voyager catalog. Second, process the bibliographic and holdings records to produce delimited text files in the TSV format following HathiTrust specifications.

EX LIBRIS VOYAGER RESTFUL APIS

The first step was getting data out of the library's catalog, the Ex Libris Voyager database. We had used the Voyager RESTful APIs for an earlier digital project

```
let $sys-id := $marc-rec/controlfield[@tag = "001"]/string()
let $oclc-num := $marc-rec/datafield[@tag = "035"][starts-
with(., "(OCoLC)")][1]
let $rec-type := substring($marc-rec/leader, 7, 2)
let $form := substring($marc-rec/controlfield[@tag = "008"],
24, 1)
where $marc-rec
  and $oclc-num
  and ($form = " " or $form = "d" or $form = "f" or $form =
"r")
  and ($rec-type = "am" or $rec-type = "cm" or $rec-type =
"tm")
return $marc-rec
```

Figure 11.1 | **Fragment of a query for extracting MARC records for print resources**

successfully, so we decided to capture every MARC record in the database serialized as MARCXML. (Voyager's bulk export would have given us MARC21 records, but not MARCXML.) We extracted MARCXML for bibliographic, holdings, and items for all the records in our library's catalog and put them in a separate database in our digital library system, MarkLogic Server.

Figure 11.1 shows a section of the code for extracting these records. It uses XQuery to filter out the bibliographic records for nonprint resources based on fixed field codes. Another query analyzed general material designation (GMD) types, since fixed field codes are often missing. The result is a new database of print-only items with two directories, one for monographs and the other for serials. HathiTrust required three separate reports for single-part monographs, multipart monographs, and serials, each with different data submission requirements.

SERIALS

The serials submission report had the least requirements, so that was the report we tackled first. It was also the smaller dataset. Figure 11.2 shows the XQuery code that creates the HathiTrust submission file for serials. The figure illustrates all the code for creating the TSV file. We will break it down and evaluate it step-by-step.

The submission file for serials required three pieces of data: the OCLC control number, the system identifier, and, if available, the International Standard Serial Number (ISSN), as a tab separated file.

```
(: This main module creates HathiTrust submission file for serials. :)

declare namespace m = "http://www.loc.gov/MARC21/slim";

let $text := text {

  for $bib-rec in xdmp:directory("/Serials/", "infinity")

  (: Normalized and deduped OCLC numbers and remove locally added
leading zeros :)
  let $oclc-nums :=
    distinct-values(
      let $oclc-nums := $bib-rec/m:record/m:datafield[@tag =
"035"]/m:subfield[@code = "a"][starts-with(., "(OCoLC)")]
      for $oclc-num in $oclc-nums
      let $norm-string := replace($oclc-num, "^\D*(\d+)\s*$", "$1")
      let $norm-num :=
        if ($norm-string = "(OCoLC)") then () else $norm-string
      where $norm-num != ""
      return normalize-space($norm-num))

  let $sys-id := normalize-space($bib-rec/m:record/m:controlfield[@tag
= "001"])
  let $tab := "&#09;"
  let $new-line := "&#10;"

  let $issn-num :=
    normalize-space(distinct-values($bib-rec/m:record/m:datafield[@tag
= "022"]/m:subfield[@code = "a"]))

  order by $sys-id

  return
    if (count($oclc-nums) = 1) then
      concat($oclc-nums, $tab, $sys-id, $tab, $issn-num, $new-line)
    else if (count($oclc-nums) > 1) then
          concat(string-join($oclc-nums, ","), $tab, $sys-id, $tab,
$issn-num, $new-line)
         else () }

return xdmp:save("C:\Program Files\MarkLogic\ptsem_serials_20160613.
tsv", $text)
```

Figure 11.2 | **Main module that creates HathiTrust submission file for serials**

The first part of the query extracts the OCLC control numbers. This code has several steps to get the numbers in the form necessary for the report. It queries the 035 fields, looking for those that start with "(OCoLC)": `$oclc-nums := $bib-rec/m:record/m:datafield[@tag = "035"]/m:subfield[@code = "a"][starts-with(., "(OCoLC)")]`

Next, it normalizes the OCLC number string by extracting only the numeric portion using a regular expression:[1] `let $norm-string := replace($oclc-num, "^\D*(\d+)\s*$", "$1")`

Another step for normalizing the OCLC number is needed due to local anomalies. Some bibliographic records have the OCLC prefix but no number. So, the code tests for these and filters them out.

```
let $norm-num :=

if ($norm-string = "(OCoLC)") then () else
$norm-string

where $norm-num != ""

return normalize-space($norm-num)
```

Finally, our local bibliographic records will sometimes contain duplicate OCLC control numbers. So, that part of the query also uses the distinct-values() function to de-duplicate the return value. The result is a sequence of unique OCLC control numbers assigned to the variable `$oclc-nums`.

The Voyager system identifier is a much simpler data extraction. It is basically XPath navigation to the 001 field and the normalize-space() function to remove any extraneous whitespace: `let $sys-id := normalize-space($bib-rec/m:record/m:controlfield[@tag = "001"])`.

> Similarly, the ISSN is extracted and de-duped: `let $issn-num := normalize-space(distinct-values($bib-rec/m:record/m:datafield[@tag = "022"]/m:subfield[@code = "a"]))`

Variables are set up for tab and newline characters that will be needed in the return clause to build the file. Using the order by clause of the FLWOR expression, we order the result by the system identifier.

Now we are ready for the final set. The return clause contains a conditional expression (if/then/else). This is needed to test for records where there is more than one OCLC number with different values. These multiple OCLC numbers are to be included in the file for the HathiTrust separated by commas.

```
return
if (count($oclc-nums) = 1) then
concat($oclc-nums, $tab, $sys-id, $tab, $issn-num,
$new-line)
else if (count($oclc-nums) > 1) then
concat(string-join($oclc-nums, ","), $tab, $sys-id,
$tab, $issn-num, $new-line)
else () }
```

All the code described so far is assigned to a variable named `$text`. We now have everything we need for the TSV file, so when we return the text file, we just need to name the new file and save it to the file system: `return xdmp:save("C:\Program Files\MarkLogic\ptsem_serials _20160613.tsv", $text)`

You may have noticed that many of the functions discussed earlier in this book are used in this query.

SINGLE-PART MONOGRAPHS

The next file that we worked on for this project was for print monographs that are single-part items. The values needed by HathiTrust for this file were OCLC numbers and system identifiers. Of course, the database had a single directory for monographic items, so we had to filter out the multipart monographs when processing the records. This was achieved by writing a user-defined function, get-volume-info(), to test for volume information and exclude it from the results. The code for this part of the project was complex due to the fact that our volume information was in different fields: both the 866 and 899 of the holdings record and the enumeration field of the Voyager item record for circulating materials. Also, the 866 contained summary holdings, for example, v.1–3, so the number range had to be expanded to create a single listing for each volume required for the submission of the HathiTrust report. A separate function was written just for that one step and was named expand-866-field().

There is also a separate function that got volume information from the Voyager item record from a field called "enumeration." The user-defined function was called get-enumeration(). After analysis, it was discovered that some of the data in this field was incorrect. For some records, copy numbers had been put in the field by mistake. So those were filtered out: `let $enums :=`

```
$items/itemData[@name = "enumeration"][not(starts-with(.,
"c"))][. != ""]
```

There was a third use-defined function that was created to extract "number" and "part" as well as "year" for annuals. This function was called get-other-enumerations(). You can see from the main function get-volume-info() that all three functions just discussed are called within the main function. This is a good example of how functions can control code complexity (see figure 11.3).

```
(: Gets the 866 or 899 fields of the holdings record for volume
information :)
declare function mpm:get-volume-info($seq as xs:integer)
as xs:string*
{
let $records := xdmp:directory(concat("/Monographs/", $seq, "/"),
"infinity")
let $holdings := $records/holdings/institution/holding
for $holding in $holdings (: Can be more than one holdings record :)
(: First 866 field is generally volume information :)
let $_866 := $holding/marcRecord/datafield[@tag = "866"][1]/subfield[@
code = "a"]
let $_899s := $holding/marcRecord/datafield[@tag = "899"]/subfield[@code
= "a"]
let $enums := mpm:get-enumeration($seq)
let $_866-vols := mpm:expand-866-field($seq)
let $vols :=
  if ($_899s) then
    for $_899 in $_899s
    return normalize-space($_899)
  else if ($_866 and starts-with ($_866, "v.")) then
         mpm:expand-866-field($seq)
        else if ($_866 and not(starts-with ($_866, "v."))) then
               mpm:get-other-enumerations($seq)
             else ()

where not($enums)
return $vols
};
```

Figure 11.3 | **User-defined function that extracts volume information from the holdings record**

MULTIPART MONOGRAPHS

The third and final TSV file needed for this project was for the multipart monographs. We have already discussed some of the XQuery code to work with the extraction of volume information. The HathiTrust report required the volume designations to be part of the report. Since we had volume information in multiple places, we had to make a judgment call as to where the volume information was most accurate and easiest to extract. The decision was made to use the enumeration field of the item records when available. Otherwise, the volume information would come from the holdings records from either the 866 or 899 field.

CONCLUSION

All of the XQuery code for this HathiTrust project is available at http://github.com/caschwartz. The complete modules are there for evaluation and reuse. This chapter is meant to show a real-world example of using XQuery to query a large dataset, analyze it, and extract metadata from various locations. This practical example shows how the power of XQuery can make library metadata work more efficient.

Note

1. We could have left in the various OCLC prefixes, but chose not to.

RESOURCES FOR FURTHER STUDY

Chapters 2 to 11 have introduced detailed XML, XPath, XQuery, and other related technologies, as well as practical examples of how these technologies are used in the library. However, there are other resources and courses that cataloging and metadata professionals and developers can use to further hone their technical skills. This chapter tries to share available resources, web courses, and links for web standards and technologies that are relevant to cataloging and metadata workflows.

TUTORIALS AND COURSES

There are a host of XML and XML-related courses available, as given below. Please keep in mind that some require fees.

- Library Juice Academy: http://libraryjuiceacademy.com/certificate-xml-rdf.php
- Coursera: https://www.coursera.org/

- Free Webmaster Help
    - XML: www.freewebmasterhelp.com/tutorials/xml
    - XHTML: www.freewebmasterhelp.com/tutorials/xhtml
        - Perfect XML
            - XML: www.perfectxml.com/articles/xml/begin.asp
            - XQuery: www.perfectxml.com/linkquery.asp
        - Tzag.com
            - XML: www.tizag.com/xmlTutorial/index.php
            - XPath: www.tizag.com/xmlTutorial/xpathtutorial.php
            - XSLT: www.tizag.com/xmlTutorial/xslttutorial.php
        - Tutorials Point
            - XML: https://www.tutorialspoint.com/xml/
            - XPath: www.tutorialspoint.com/xpath/
            - XQuery: www.tutorialspoint.com/xquery/
            - XSLT: www.tutorialspoint.com/xslt/
        - W3 Schools
            - XML: www.w3schools.com/xml/
            - XPath: www.w3schools.com/xml/xpath_intro.asp
            - XQuery: www.w3schools.com/xml/xquery_intro.asp
            - XSLT: www.w3schools.com/xml/xsl_intro.asp

KNOWLEDGE BASES AND READY REFERENCES

This section provides links to places where librarians and programmers share their workflows and associated programs, as well as ready references for elements and functions that are useful when creating XQueries and XSLTs.

- IBM developerWorks: https://www.ibm.com/developerworks/xml/tutorials/x-introxslt/x-introxslt-pdf.pdf
- Cover Pages:
    - XSLT: http://xml.coverpages.org/xsl.html
    - XML & XQuery: http://xml.coverpages.org/xmlQuery.html

- Learn XQuery: A list of great articles, blog posts, and books for learning XQuery: http://github.com/joewiz/learnxquery
- Lenz Consulting: http://lenzconsulting.com/resources/
- Library Workflow Exchange: www.libraryworkflowexchange.org/about/
- Stack Overflow: http://stackoverflow.com/
- W3 Schools
  - XSLT Elements Reference: www.w3schools.com/xml/xsl_elementref.asp
  - XSLT, XPath, and XQuery Functions: www.w3schools.com/xml/xsl_functions.asp
- XML.com
  - XML: https://www.xml.com/articles/2017/01/01/xmlcom-redux/
  - XSLT: https://www.xml.com/articles/2017/01/01/what-is-xslt/
- XQuery Wikibook: http://en.wikibooks.org/wiki/XQuery
- XQuery Power: A list of resources built on or with XQuery
  - http://github.com/joewiz/xquerypower
- FunctX XQuery Functions: www.xqueryfunctions.com

TOOLS

Tools such as XML editors, debuggers, and testers help make metadata creation and transformation relatively easy. Please pay attention to the utility of each tool and its required system support before downloading and using one.

- XPath Testers
  - XPath Tester: www.xpathtester.com/xpath
  - Freeformatter: www.freeformatter.com/xpath-tester.html
  - Code Beauty: http://codebeautify.org/Xpath-Tester
- XML Editors & XSLT Debuggers
  - Freeformatter
    - www.freeformatter.com/xsl-transformer.html
    - www.freeformatter.com/xml-validator-xsd.html

- oXygen: https://www.oxygenxml.com/
- Altova: https://www.altova.com/
- Stylus Studio: www.stylusstudio.com/
- Liquid XML Studio: https://www.liquid-technologies.com/
- MarcEdit: http://marcedit.reeset.net/downloads

METADATA SCHEMA LOCATIONS

Creating valid XML document and functioning XSLTs requires correct schema locations in the document. Metadata schemas heavily used in the library domain are the following:

- CDWA-Lite: www.getty.edu/CDWA/CDWALite/CDWALite-xsd-public-v1–1.xsd
- Darwin Core: http://rs.tdwg.org/dwc/xsd/tdwg_dwc_simple.xsd
- Dublin Core
    - http://purl.org/dc/elements/1.1/
    - OAI-DC: www.openarchives.org/OAI/2.0/oai_dc/
    - http://dublincore.org/schemas/xmls/qdc/2008/02/11/dc.xsd
    - http://dublincore.org/schemas/xmls/qdc/2008/02/11/dcterms.xsd
    - http://dublincore.org/schemas/xmls/qdc/2008/02/11/simpledc.xsd
    - http://dublincore.org/schemas/xmls/qdc/2008/02/11/qualifieddc.xsd
- EAD
    - RNG: https://www.loc.gov/ead/ead3.rng
    - XSD: https://www.loc.gov/ead/ead3.xsd
    - DTD: https://www.loc.gov/ead/ead3.dtd
- MARC: https://www.loc.gov/standards/marcxml/schema/MARC21slim.xsd
- METS: www.loc.gov/standards/mets/mets.xsd
- Metadata for Images in XML (MIS): www.loc.gov/standards/mix/mix.xsd

- MODS (all versions): www.loc.gov/standards/mods/mods-schemas.html
- PBCore 2.1: https://raw.githubusercontent.com/WGBH/PBCore_2.1/master/pbcore-2.1.xsd
- PREMIS 3.0: www.loc.gov/standards/premis/premis.xsd
- TEI
  - All: https://www.tei-c.org/release/xml/tei/custom/schema/xsd/tei_all.xsd
  - Lite: https://www.tei-c.org/release/xml/tei/custom/schema/xsd/tei_lite.xsd
  - Bare: https://www.tei-c.org/release/xml/tei/custom/schema/xsd/tei_bare.xsd
- Texas Digital Library ETD: www.ndltd.org/standards/metadata/etdms/1–0/etdms.xsd
- VRA Core 4.0
  - https://www.loc.gov/standards/vracore/vra.xsd
  - https://www.loc.gov/standards/vracore/vra-strict.xsd

CROSSWALKS BETWEEN METADATA STANDARDS

Transformation between two different standards starts from the mapping/crosswalking process. Several metadata standards provides crosswalking documents to other metadata standards.

- CDWA to other metadata standards: www.getty.edu/research/publications/electronic_publications/intrometadata/crosswalks.html
- Dublin Core to MARC21: https://www.loc.gov/marc/dccross.html
- Dublin Core to MODS Version 3: www.loc.gov/standards/mods/dcsimple-mods.html
- MARC21 to Dublin Core: https://www.loc.gov/marc/marc2dc.html
- MARC 21 to MODS 3.6: https://www.loc.gov/standards/mods/mods-mapping.html
- MODS 3.5 to MARC 21: www.loc.gov/standards/mods/v3/mods2marc-mapping.html
- MODS Version 3 to Dublin Core: www.loc.gov/standards/mods/mods-dcsimple.html

- TEI Header to MARC21: www.tei-c.org/SIG/Libraries/teiinlibraries/main-driver.html#index.xml-body.1_div.4_div.1_div.3
- VRA Core to MARC21: https://www.loc.gov/standards/vracore/VRACore3_MapToMarc.pdf

BOOKS

Anderson, Clifford B., Jonathan Robie, and Joseph C. Wicentowski. *XQuery for Humanists: Coding for Humanists*. College Station, TX: Texas A&M Press, forthcoming.

Brundage, Michael. *XQuery: The XML Query Language*. Boston: Addison-Wesley, 2004.

Cole, Timothy W., and Myung-Ja K. Han. *XML for Catalogers and Metadata Librarians*. Third Millennium Cataloging Series. Santa Barbara, CA: Libraries Unlimited, 2013.

Fitzgerald, Michael. *Learning XSLT: A Hands-On Introduction to XSLT and XPath*. Sebastopol, CA: O'Reilly, 2003.

Harold, Elliotte Rusty, and W. Scott Means. *XML in a Nutshell.* 3rd edition. Sebastopol, CA: O'Reilly Media, 2004.

Hitchens, Ron. *Getting Started with XQuery: Query XML Like You Mean It.* Raleigh, NC: Pragmatic Bookshelf, 2008. (This is a PDF publication.)

Katz, Howard, ed. *XQuery from the Experts: A Guide to the W3C XML Query Language*. Boston: Addison-Wesley, 2004.

Kay, Michael. *XSLT 2.0 and XPath 2.0: Programmer's Reference.* 4th edition. Indianapolis, IN: Wiley Publishing, 2008.

Kelly, David James. *XSLT Jumpstarter: Level the Learning Curve and Put Your XML to Work*. Raleigh, NC: Peloria, 2015.

McCreary, Dan, and Ann Kelly. *Making Sense of NoSQL: A Guide for Managers and the Rest of Us.* Manning, 2013. (While primarily a book on NoSQL databases, chapter 5 is devoted to native XML databases and discusses topics relevant to this text: XML, XQuery, and XML Schema.)

Melton, Jim, and Stephen Buxton. *Querying XML: XQuery, XPath, and SQL/XML in Context.* San Francisco: Morgan Kaufmann, 2006.

Ray, Erik T. *Learning XML.* 2nd edition. Sebastopol, CA: O'Reilly Media, 2003.

Simpson, John E. *XPath and XPointer.* Sebastopol, CA: O'Reilly & Associates, 2002.

Tidwell, Doug. *XSLT: Mastering XML Transformations.* 2nd edition. Sebastopol, CA: O'Reilly Media, 2008.

Walmsley, Priscilla. *Definitive XML Schema.* 2nd edition. Charles F. Goldfarb Definitive XML Series. Upper Saddle River, NJ: Prentice Hall, 2013.

———. *XQuery: Search across a Variety of XML Data.* 2nd edition. Sebastopol, CA: O'Reilly Media, 2016.

APPENDIX

Sample SPINE Metadata Record for an Emblem Book

(discussed in chapter 7)

```
<?xml version="1.0" encoding="UTF-8"?>
<biblioDesc xmlns="http://diglib.hab.de/rules/schema/emblem"
xmlns:xsi="http://www.w3.org/2001/XMLSchema-instance"
xsi:schemaLocation="http://www.loc.gov/mods/v3 http://www.loc.gov/
standards/mods/mods.xsd
http://diglib.hab.de/rules/schema/emblem http://diglib.hab.de/rules/
schema/emblem/emblem-1-2.xsd"
xmlns:rdf="http://www.w3.org/1999/02/22-rdf-syntax-ns#"
xmlns:skos="http://www.w3.org/2004/02/skos/core#">
<mods:mods xmlns:rdf="http://www.w3.org/1999/02/22-rdf-syntax-ns#"
xmlns:skos="http://www.w3.org/2004/02/skos/core#"
xmlns:mods="http://www.loc.gov/mods/v3"
xmlns:tei="http://www.tei-c.org/ns/1.0"
xmlns:xlink="http://www.w3.org/1999/xlink"
version="3.4">
<mods:titleInfo>
<mods:title>Meditationes emblematicae de restaurata pace Germaniae =</
mods:title>
<mods:subTitle>Sinnebilder von dem widergebrachten Teutschen Frieden</
mods:subTitle>
</mods:titleInfo>
<mods:titleInfo type="alternative">
<mods:title>Sinnebilder von dem widergebrachten Teutschen Frieden</
mods:title>
</mods:titleInfo>
<mods:titleInfo type="alternative">
<mods:title>Meditationes de restaurata pace</mods:title>
</mods:titleInfo>
<mods:titleInfo type="alternative">
```

```
<mods:title>Sinnbilder von dem wiedergebrachten Frieden in
Teutschlandt</mods:title>
</mods:titleInfo>
<mods:name type=”personal”>
<mods:namePart>Vogel, Johann</mods:namePart>
<mods:namePart type=”date”>1589-1663</mods:namePart>
<mods:role>
<mods:roleTerm authority=”marcrelator” type=”text”>creator</
mods:roleTerm>
</mods:role>
</mods:name>
<mods:name type=”personal”>
<mods:namePart>Zunner, Johann David</mods:namePart>
<mods:namePart type=”date”>d. 1653</mods:namePart>
<mods:role>
<mods:roleTerm type=”text”>printer.</mods:roleTerm>
</mods:role>
</mods:name>
<mods:typeOfResource>text</mods:typeOfResource>
<mods:genre authority=”rbgenr”>Emblem books-Germany-17th century.</
mods:genre>
<mods:originInfo>
<mods:place>
<mods:placeTerm type=”code” authority=”marccountry”>gw</
mods:placeTerm>
</mods:place>
<mods:place>
<mods:placeTerm type=”text”>Francofurti</mods:placeTerm>
</mods:place>
<mods:publisher>Apud Joh. Dav. Zunnerum</mods:publisher>
<mods:dateIssued>[1649]</mods:dateIssued>
<mods:issuance>monographic</mods:issuance>
</mods:originInfo>
<mods:language>
<mods:languageTerm authority=”iso639-2b” type=”code”>lat</
mods:languageTerm>
</mods:language>
<mods:language>
<mods:languageTerm authority=”iso639-2b” type=”code”>ger</
mods:languageTerm>
</mods:language>
<mods:physicalDescription>
<mods:digitalOrigin>reformatted digital</mods:digitalOrigin>
<mods:form authority=”marcform”>print</mods:form>
<mods:extent>[5], XXIV, XXIV, [3] p. : ill. (engravings) ; 22 cm
(4to)</mods:extent>
```

```
</mods:physicalDescription>
<mods:note type=”statement of responsibility”>k&#x00FC;rzlich
erkl&#x00E4;rt durch Johann Vogel.</mods:note>
<mods:note>Publication date appears as chronogram on title-page.</
mods:note>
<mods:note>Place of publication and printer from additional engraved
title-page: “Meditationes de restaurata pace = Sinnbilder von dem
wiedergebrachten Frieden in Teutschlandt / Johannis Vogelij,” with
imprint: “Francofurti : Apud Joh. Dav. Zunnerum.”</mods:note>
<mods:note>Opposite pages bear duplicate numbering.</mods:note>
<mods:note>Signatures: A-G.</mods:note>
<mods:note>Added title-page has ornamental border; initials; head-
pieces; [24] engraved emblems.</mods:note>
<mods:note>”1649” inscribed in ink on title-page.</mods:note>
<mods:note type=”language”>Text in Latin and German.</mods:note>
<mods:subject authority=”lcsh”>
<mods:topic>Emblems</mods:topic>
<mods:genre>Early works to 1800</mods:genre>
</mods:subject>
<mods:subject authority=”lcsh”>
<mods:topic>Emblem books, Latin</mods:topic>
<mods:geographic>Germany</mods:geographic>
<mods:temporal>17th century</mods:temporal>
</mods:subject>
<mods:subject authority=”lcsh”>
<mods:topic>Emblem books, German</mods:topic>
<mods:geographic>Germany</mods:geographic>
<mods:temporal>17th century</mods:temporal>
</mods:subject>
<mods:location>
<mods:url displayLabel=”Full text—UIUC” usage=”primary
display”>http://hdl.handle.net/10111/UIUCOCA:meditationesemb100voge</
mods:url>
</mods:location>
<mods:location>
<mods:url displayLabel=”Full text—OCA”>http://www.archive.org/details/
meditationesemb100voge</mods:url>
</mods:location>
<mods:location>
<mods:url displayLabel=”Full text—Arkyves”>http://www.arkyves.org/uid/
uiuc_5676683</mods:url>
</mods:location>
<mods:location>
<mods:url displayLabel=”Mets Navigator”>http://libsysdigi.
library.illinois.edu/oca/Books2009-11/meditationesemb100voge/
meditationesemb100voge.xml</mods:url>
```

```
</mods:location>
<mods:recordInfo>
<mods:descriptionStandard>aacr2</mods:descriptionStandard>
<mods:descriptionStandard>rakwb</mods:descriptionStandard>
<mods:recordContentSource authority=”marcorg”>GyGoGBV</
mods:recordContentSource>
<mods:recordCreationDate encoding=”marc”>070710</
mods:recordCreationDate>
<mods:recordChangeDate encoding=”iso8601”>20100830160116.0</
mods:recordChangeDate>
<mods:recordIdentifier>5676683</mods:recordIdentifier>
<mods:recordOrigin>Converted from MARCXML to MODS version 3.3 using
MARC21slim2MODS3-3.xsl (Revision 1.54)</mods:recordOrigin>
<mods:languageOfCataloging>
<mods:languageTerm authority=”iso639-2b” type=”code”>ger</
mods:languageTerm>
</mods:languageOfCataloging>
</mods:recordInfo>
<mods:genre authority=”aat” type=”concept” valueURI=”http://vocab.
getty.edu/aat/300026286” >emblem books</mods:genre>
<mods:identifier type=”LGM” displayLabel=”Landwehr, J. German emblem
books”>628</mods:identifier>
<mods:identifier type=”MN” displayLabel=”McGeary &amp; Nash. Emblem
books at the University of Illinois”>V36</mods:identifier>
<mods:identifier type=”vd17” displayLabel=”VD 17 (online)”>23:000260P</
mods:identifier>
</mods:mods>
<copyDesc>
<copyID>uiu5676683</copyID>
<owner countryCode=”US”>University of Illinois</owner>
<digDesc comp=”complete” scope=”all” xml:id=”meditationesemb100voge”
globalID=”http://hdl.handle.net/10111/UIUCOCA:meditationesemb100voge”
pageImages=”http://emblemimages.grainger.illinois.edu/
meditationesemb100voge/meditationesemb100voge_jp2.zip”>Digital RGB
(8 bit x 3) color facsimile scanned at between 300 and 500 dpi by
the Open Content Alliance on an OCA Scribe workstation (Canon 5D)
at the University of Illinois at Urbana-Champaign. <copyID>10111/
UIUCOCA:meditationesemb100voge</copyID>
<owner countryCode=”US”>University of Illinois</owner>
</digDesc>
<digDesc comp=”complete” scope=”all” globalID=”http://www.archive.
org/details/meditationesemb100voge”>View in Internet Archive
<copyID>meditationesemb100voge</copyID>
<owner countryCode=”US”>Internet Archive</owner>
</digDesc>
<digDesc comp=”complete” scope=”all” globalID=”http://www.arkyves.org/
```

```
uid/uiuc_5676683”>View in Arkyves <copyID>uiuc_5676683</copyID>
<owner countryCode=”NL”>Arkyves</owner>
</digDesc>
</copyDesc>
<emblem xmlns:xlink=”http://www.w3.org/1999/xlink” citeNo=”I.”
xlink:href=”http://djatoka.grainger.illinois.edu/index.
html?url=http://emblemimages.grainger.illinois.edu/
meditationesemb100voge/JP2Processed/meditationesemb100voge_0010-0011.
jp2&amp;crop=false” xml:id=”E000001” globalID=”http://hdl.handle.
net/10111/EmblemRegistry:E000001”>
<motto>
<transcription xml:lang=”de”>Hie sol nun seyn de&#x00DF; Krieges Ziel.
<normalisation xml:lang=”de”>Hier soll nun des Krieges Ziel sein.</
normalisation>
</transcription>
<transcription xml:lang=”la”>Hic belli terminus esto.</transcription>
</motto>
<pictura xlink:href=”http://djatoka.grainger.illinois.edu/adore-
djatoka/resolver?url_ver=Z39.88-2004&amp;rft_id=http://emblemimages.
grainger.illinois.edu/meditationesemb100voge/JP2Processed/
meditationesemb100voge_0010-0011.jp2&amp;svc_id=info:lanl-repo/svc/
getRegion&amp;svc_val_fmt=info:ofi/fmt:kev:mtx:jpeg2000&amp;svc.
format=image/jpeg&amp;svc.level=5&amp;svc.rotate=0&amp;svc.
region=768,2832,1440,1240” xml:id=”E000001_P1”>
<iconclass rdf:about=”http://www.iconclass.org/rkd/22C11”>
<skos:notation>22C11</skos:notation>
<skos:prefLabel>rays of natural light</skos:prefLabel>
</iconclass>
<iconclass rdf:about=”http://www.iconclass.org/rkd/25H1124”>
<skos:notation>25H1124</skos:notation>
<skos:prefLabel>boulder, stone</skos:prefLabel>
</iconclass>
<iconclass rdf:about=”http://www.iconclass.org/rkd/45A20”>
<skos:notation>45A20</skos:notation>
<skos:prefLabel>symbols, allegories of peace, ‘Pax’; ‘Pace’ (Ripa)</
skos:prefLabel>
</iconclass>
<iconclass rdf:about=”http://www.iconclass.org/rkd/61A(1649)”>
<skos:notation>61A( . . . )</skos:notation>
<skos:prefLabel>historical events and situations (with DATE)</
skos:prefLabel>
</iconclass>
<iconclass  rdf:about=”http://www.iconclass.org/rkd/61K(THIRTY  YEARS’
WAR)”>
<skos:notation>61K( . . . )</skos:notation>
<skos:prefLabel>(other) historical names (with NAME)</skos:prefLabel>
```

```
</iconclass>
<iconclass rdf:about="http://www.iconclass.org/rkd/86(HIC BELLI
TERMINUS ESTO)">
<skos:notation>86( . . . )</skos:notation>
<skos:prefLabel>proverbs, sayings, etc. (with TEXT)</skos:prefLabel>
</iconclass>
<iconclass rdf:about="http://www.iconclass.org/rkd/86(HIER SOLL NUN
DES KRIEGES ZIEL SEIN)">
<skos:notation>86( . . . ) </skos:notation>
<skos:prefLabel>proverbs, sayings, etc. (with TEXT)</skos:prefLabel>
</iconclass>
<iconclass rdf:about="http://www.iconclass.org/rkd/96A16">
<skos:notation>96A16</skos:notation>
<skos:prefLabel>Terminus</skos:prefLabel>
</iconclass>
</pictura>
</emblem>
<!—Descriptions of additional emblems removed for brevity—>
</biblioDesc>
```

APPENDIX

XSLT for Creating Book-Level HTML+RDFa

(discussed in chapter 7)

```
<?xml version="1.0" encoding="UTF-8"?>
<xsl:stylesheet xmlns:xsl="http://www.w3.org/1999/XSL/Transform"
xmlns:xsi="http://www.w3.org/2001/XMLSchema-instance"
xmlns:html="http://www.w3.org/1999/xhtml"
xmlns:xlink="http://www.w3.org/1999/xlink" version="1.0"
xmlns:mods="http://www.loc.gov/mods/v3"
xmlns:spine="http://diglib.hab.de/rules/schema/emblem"
exclude-result-prefixes="xsl xsi html xlink mods spine">
<xsl:output method="xml" encoding="UTF-8" indent="yes" omit-xml-
declaration="yes"/>
<xsl:variable name="BookUri">
<xsl:choose>
<xsl:when test="/spine:biblioDesc/mods:mods/mods:location/mods:url/@
usage='primary display'">
<xsl:value-of select="/spine:biblioDesc/mods:mods/mods:location/
mods:url[@usage='primary display']"/>
</xsl:when>
<xsl:when test="//mods:mods/mods:identifier/@type='purl'">
<xsl:value-of select="//mods:mods/mods:identifier[@type='purl']"/>
</xsl:when>
<xsl:when test="//mods:mods/mods:location/mods:url">
<xsl:value-of select="//mods:mods/mods:location/mods:url"/>
</xsl:when>
</xsl:choose>
</xsl:variable>
<xsl:template match="/">
<xsl:text disable-output-escaping="yes">&lt;!DOCTYPE html&gt;&#0010;</
xsl:text>
<html>
<head>
```

```
<title>Book Information</title>
<meta charset="UTF-8"/>
<style type="text/css">
.table { display: table; padding: 7px; }
.row { display: table-row; }
.col-sm-3 { display: table-cell; padding: 7px; width: 25%; }
.col-sm-9 { display: table-cell; padding: 7px; }
ul { padding-left:17px; }
</style>
</head>
<body>
<xsl:apply-templates select="//mods:mods"/>
</body>
</html>
</xsl:template>
<xsl:template match="mods:mods">
<div class="table" prefix="s: http://schema.org/" typeof="s:Book"
resource="{$BookUri}">
<meta property="s:additionalType" content="http://schema.org/
Product"/>
<div class="row">
<div class="col-sm-3">
<span>
<b>Title</b>
</span>
</div>
<div class="col-sm-9">
<span property="s:name">
<xsl:value-of select="mods:titleInfo/mods:title"/>
<xsl:value-of select="mods:titleInfo/mods:subTitle"/>
</span>
</div>
</div>
<xsl:if test="mods:name">
<div class="row">
<div class="col-sm-3">
<span>
<b>Authors and contributors</b>
</span>
</div>
<div class="col-sm-9">
<ul>
<xsl:for-each select="mods:name">
<xsl:element name="li">
<xsl:attribute name="class">name</xsl:attribute>
<xsl:choose>
```

```
<xsl:when test="position()=1">
<!—arguably we should test for usage="primary"—>
<xsl:attribute name="property">s:author</xsl:attribute>
</xsl:when>
<xsl:otherwise>
<xsl:attribute name="property">s:contributor</xsl:attribute>
</xsl:otherwise>
</xsl:choose>
<xsl:choose>
<xsl:when test="./@type='personal'">
<xsl:attribute name="typeof">s:Person</xsl:attribute>
</xsl:when>
<xsl:otherwise>
<xsl:attribute name="typeof">s:Organization</xsl:attribute>
</xsl:otherwise>
</xsl:choose>
<xsl:if test="./@valueURI">
<xsl:attribute name="resource">
<xsl:value-of select="./@valueURI"/>
</xsl:attribute>
</xsl:if>
<xsl:element name="span">
<xsl:if test="not(./@valueURI)">
<xsl:attribute name="property">s:name</xsl:attribute>
</xsl:if>
<xsl:value-of select="mods:namePart[1]"/>
<xsl:if test="mods:namePart[2]">
<xsl:text>, </xsl:text>
<xsl:value-of select="mods:namePart[2]"/>
</xsl:if>
<xsl:text>. </xsl:text>
</xsl:element>
<xsl:if test="./mods:role/mods:roleTerm">
<xsl:element name="span">
<xsl:attribute name="property">s:jobTitle</xsl:attribute>
<xsl:value-of select="./mods:role/mods:roleTerm"/>
</xsl:element>
</xsl:if>
</xsl:element>
</xsl:for-each>
</ul>
</div>
</div>
</xsl:if>
<xsl:if test="mods:originInfo/mods:publisher">
<div class="row">
```

```
<div class="col-sm-3">
<span>
<b>Publisher</b>
</span>
</div>
<div class="col-sm-9" property="s:publisher" typeof="s:Organization">
<span property="s:name">
<xsl:value-of select="mods:originInfo/mods:publisher"/>
</span>
</div>
</div>
</xsl:if>
<xsl:for-each select="mods:originInfo/mods:place/mods:placeTerm">
<xsl:choose>
<xsl:when test="./@type='code'">
<xsl:text>&#0010;</xsl:text>
<xsl:element name="span">
<xsl:attribute name="style">display:none</xsl:attribute>
<xsl:attribute name="property">s:locationCreated</xsl:attribute>
<xsl:if test="./@valueURI">
<xsl:attribute name="resource">
<xsl:value-of select="./@valueURI"/>
</xsl:attribute>
<xsl:attribute name="typeof">s:Place</xsl:attribute>
</xsl:if>
<xsl:value-of select="."/>
</xsl:element>
<xsl:text>&#0010;</xsl:text>
</xsl:when>
<xsl:otherwise>
<div class="row">
<div class="col-sm-3">
<span>
<b>Place of Publication</b>
</span>
</div>
<div class="col-sm-9">
<xsl:element name="span">
<xsl:attribute name="property">s:locationCreated</xsl:attribute>
<xsl:if test="./@valueURI">
<xsl:attribute name="resource">
<xsl:value-of select="./@valueURI"/>
</xsl:attribute>
<xsl:attribute name="typeof">s:Place</xsl:attribute>
</xsl:if>
<xsl:value-of select="."/>
```

```
</xsl:element>
</div>
</div>
</xsl:otherwise>
</xsl:choose>
</xsl:for-each>
<xsl:if test="mods:originInfo/mods:dateIssued">
<xsl:variable name="dateIssuedValue">
<xsl:value-of select="mods:originInfo/mods:dateIssued"/>
</xsl:variable>
<div class="row">
<div class="col-sm-3">
<span>
<b>Publication Date</b>
</span>
</div>
<div class="col-sm-9">
<span property="s:datePublished" content="{$dateIssuedValue}">
<xsl:value-of select="mods:originInfo/mods:dateIssued"/>
</span>
</div>
</div>
</xsl:if>
<xsl:if test="mods:physicalDescription">
<div class="row">
<div class="col-sm-3">
<span>
<b>Physical Description</b>
</span>
</div>
<div class="col-sm-9">
<xsl:choose>
<xsl:when test="count(mods:physicalDescription) = 1">
<span property="s:description">
<xsl:value-of select="normalize-space(mods:physicalDescription)"/>
</span>
</xsl:when>
<xsl:otherwise>
<ul>
<xsl:for-each select="mods:physicalDescription">
<xsl:for-each select="./*">
<li property="s:description">
<xsl:value-of select="normalize-space(.)"/>
</li>
</xsl:for-each>
</xsl:for-each>
```

```
</ul>
</xsl:otherwise>
</xsl:choose>
</div>
</div>
</xsl:if>
<xsl:if test="mods:language/mods:languageTerm">
<div class="row">
<div class="col-sm-3">
<span>
<b>Language</b>
</span>
</div>
<div class="col-sm-9">
<ul>
<xsl:for-each select="mods:language/mods:languageTerm">
<xsl:variable name="LangUri">http://id.loc.gov/vocabulary/is0639-
2/<xsl:value-of
select="."/></xsl:variable>
<li property="s:inLanguage" resource="{$LangUri}" typeof="s:Language">
<xsl:value-of select="."/>
</li>
</xsl:for-each>
</ul>
</div>
</div>
</xsl:if>
<xsl:if test="mods:subject">
<div class="row">
<div class="col-sm-3">
<span>
<b>Subjects</b>
</span>
</div>
<div class="col-sm-9">
<ul>
<xsl:for-each select="mods:subject">
<xsl:element name="li">
<xsl:attribute name="property">s:about</xsl:attribute>
<xsl:choose>
<xsl:when test="local-name(./child::*[1])='name'">
<xsl:choose>
<xsl:when test="./mods:name/@valueURI">
<xsl:attribute name="resource">
<xsl:value-of select="./mods:name/@valueURI"/>
</xsl:attribute>
```

```
<xsl:choose>
<xsl:when test="./mods:name/@type='personal'">
<xsl:attribute name="typeof">s:Person</xsl:attribute>
</xsl:when>
<xsl:otherwise>
<xsl:attribute name="typeof">s:Organization</xsl:attribute>
</xsl:otherwise>
</xsl:choose>
<xsl:for-each select="./mods:name/child::*">
<xsl:value-of select="."/>
<xsl:if test="position()!=last()">
<xsl:text> </xsl:text>
</xsl:if>
</xsl:for-each>
</xsl:when>
<xsl:otherwise>
<xsl:for-each select="./mods:name/child::*">
<xsl:value-of select="."/>
<xsl:if test="position()!=last()">
<xsl:text> </xsl:text>
</xsl:if>
</xsl:for-each>
</xsl:otherwise>
</xsl:choose>
</xsl:when>
<xsl:when test="local-name(./child::*[1])='hierarchicalGeographic'">
<xsl:if test="./mods:hierarchicalGeographic/@valueURI">
<xsl:attribute name="resource">
<xsl:value-of select="./mods:hierarchicalGeographic/@valueURI"/>
</xsl:attribute>
</xsl:if>
<xsl:for-each select="./mods:hierarchicalGeographic/child::*">
<xsl:value-of select="."/>
<xsl:if test="position()!=last()">
<xsl:text> </xsl:text>
</xsl:if>
</xsl:for-each>
</xsl:when>
<xsl:otherwise>
<xsl:if test="./@valueURI">
<xsl:attribute name="resource">
<xsl:value-of select="./@valueURI"/>
</xsl:attribute>
<xsl:attribute name="typeof">s:Intangible</xsl:attribute>
</xsl:if>
<xsl:for-each select="./child::*">
```

```
<xsl:value-of select="."/>
<xsl:if test="position()!=last()">
<xsl:text>–</xsl:text>
</xsl:if>
</xsl:for-each>
</xsl:otherwise>
</xsl:choose>
</xsl:element>
</xsl:for-each>
</ul>
</div>
</div>
</xsl:if>
<xsl:if test="mods:note">
<div class="row">
<div class="col-sm-3">
<span>
<b>Notes</b>
</span>
</div>
<div class="col-sm-9">
<ul>
<xsl:for-each select="mods:note">
<li property="s:description">
<xsl:value-of select="."/>
</li>
</xsl:for-each>
</ul>
</div>
</div>
</xsl:if>
<xsl:if test="mods:location/mods:url or mods:mods/mods:identifier[@
type='purl']"/>
<div class="row">
<div class="col-sm-3">
<span>
<b>Links</b>
</span>
</div>
<div class="col-sm-9">
<xsl:choose>
<xsl:when test="mods:location/mods:url">
<ul>
<xsl:for-each select="mods:location/mods:url">
<xsl:if
```

```
test="./@displayLabel != 'Full text—UIUC' and ./@displayLabel != 'Full
Text—UIUC'">
<li>
<a>
<xsl:attribute name="property">s:url</xsl:attribute>
<xsl:attribute name="href">
<xsl:value-of select="."/>
</xsl:attribute>
<xsl:choose>
<xsl:when test="./@displayLabel = 'Full text—OCA'">
<xsl:text>Internet Archive</xsl:text>
</xsl:when>
<xsl:otherwise>
<xsl:value-of select="./@displayLabel"/>
</xsl:otherwise>
</xsl:choose>
</a>
</li>
</xsl:if>
</xsl:for-each>
</ul>
</xsl:when>
<xsl:otherwise>
<ul>
<xsl:for-each select="mods:identifier[@type='purl']">
<li>
<a>
<xsl:attribute name="property">s:url</xsl:attribute>
<xsl:attribute name="href">
<xsl:value-of select="."/>
</xsl:attribute>
<xsl:value-of select="."/>
</a>
</li>
</xsl:for-each>
</ul>
</xsl:otherwise>
</xsl:choose>
</div>
</div>
</div>
</xsl:template>
</xsl:stylesheet>
```

APPENDIX

XSLT for Creating Emblem-Level HTML+RDFa

(discussed in chapter 7)

```
<?xml version="1.0" encoding="UTF-8"?>
<xsl:stylesheet xmlns:xsl="http://www.w3.org/1999/XSL/Transform"
xmlns:xsi="http://www.w3.org/2001/XMLSchema-instance"
xmlns:html="http://www.w3.org/1999/xhtml"
xmlns:xlink="http://www.w3.org/1999/xlink" version="2.0"
xmlns:mods="http://www.loc.gov/mods/v3"
xmlns:rdf="http://www.w3.org/1999/02/22-rdf-syntax-ns#"
xmlns:rdf2="http://www.w3.org/1999/02/22-rdf-syntax-ns"
xmlns:emblem="http://diglib.hab.de/rules/schema/emblem"
xmlns:skos="http://www.w3.org/2004/02/skos/core#"
exclude-result-prefixes="xsl xsi xlink html rdf rdf2 mods emblem skos">
<xsl:output method="xml" encoding="UTF-8" indent="yes" omit-xml-
declaration="yes"/>
<xsl:template match="/">
<xsl:text disable-output-escaping="yes">&lt;!DOCTYPE html&gt;&#0010;</
xsl:text>
<html>
<head>
<title>Emblem Information</title>
<meta charset="UTF-8"/>
<style type="text/css">
.table { display: table; padding: 7px; }
.row { display: table-row; }
.col-sm-3 { display: table-cell; padding: 7px; width: 25%; }
.col-sm-9 { display: table-cell; padding: 7px; }
.emptySpan { display:none; }
</style>
</head>
<body>
```

```
<xsl:apply-templates select="//emblem:emblem"/>
</body>
</html>
</xsl:template>
<xsl:template match="emblem:emblem">
<div class="table" prefix="s: http://schema.org/ e: http://emblematica.
library.illinois.edu/schemas/emb/"
typeof="s:CreativeWork">
<xsl:attribute name="resource">
<xsl:value-of select="@globalID"/>
</xsl:attribute>
<xsl:variable name="emblemID">
<xsl:value-of select="substring-after(@globalID, 'http://hdl.handle.
net/10111/EmblemRegistry:')"></xsl:value-of>
</xsl:variable>
<span class="emptySpan" property="s:additionalType" resource="http://
emblematica.library.illinois.edu/schemas/emb/Emblem"> </span>
<span class="emptySpan" property="s:sameAs"
resource="http://emblematica.library.illinois.edu/detail/emblem/
{$emblemID}"> </span>
<span class="emptySpan" property="s:associatedMedia" resource="{@
xlink:href}"> </span>
<div id="descriptors" class="row" property="s:hasPart"
typeof="s:CreativeWork">
<span class="emptySpan" property="s:additionalType" resource="http://
emblematica.library.illinois.edu/schemas/emb/Pictura"> </span>
<span class="emptySpan" property="s:associatedMedia"
resource="{emblem:pictura/@xlink:href}"> </span>
<xsl:choose>
<xsl:when test="count(emblem:pictura/emblem:iconclass) = 0">
<div class="col-sm-12">
<span class="font-20">No available descriptors for this emblem
(Iconclass Headings)</span>
</div>
</xsl:when>
<xsl:otherwise>
<div class="col-sm-3 label">
<span class="font-20">Descriptors for this Emblem (Iconclass
Headings)</span>
</div>
<div class="col-sm-9">
<xsl:for-each select="emblem:pictura/emblem:iconclass">
<xsl:element name="p">
<xsl:attribute name="class">iconclass</xsl:attribute>
<xsl:attribute name="property">s:about</xsl:attribute>
```

```
<xsl:attribute name="id">
<xsl:value-of select="concat('iconclass-,' position())"/>
</xsl:attribute>
<xsl:variable name="uriEncodedOpenParenthesis">
<xsl:call-template name="string-replace-all">
<xsl:with-param name="text" select="skos:notation" />
<xsl:with-param name="replace">(</xsl:with-param>
<xsl:with-param name="by">%28</xsl:with-param>
</xsl:call-template>
</xsl:variable>
<xsl:variable name="uriEncodedCloseParenthesis">
<xsl:call-template name="string-replace-all">
<xsl:with-param name="text" select="$uriEncodedOpenParenthesis" />
<xsl:with-param name="replace">)</xsl:with-param>
<xsl:with-param name="by">%29</xsl:with-param>
</xsl:call-template>
</xsl:variable>
<xsl:variable name="uriEncodedNotation">
<xsl:call-template name="string-replace-all">
<xsl:with-param name="text" select="$uriEncodedCloseParenthesis" />
<xsl:with-param name="replace" xml:space="preserve"> </xsl:with-param>
<xsl:with-param name="by">%20</xsl:with-param>
</xsl:call-template>
</xsl:variable>
<xsl:attribute name="resource"><xsl:value-of select="concat('http://
iconclass.org/,'$uriEncodedNotation)"/></xsl:attribute>
<xsl:value-of select="skos:notation"/>
</xsl:element>
</xsl:for-each>
</div>
</xsl:otherwise>
</xsl:choose>
</div>
<div id="motto-transcriptions" class="row">
<div class="col-sm-3 label">
<span class="font-20">Motto Transcriptions</span>
</div>
<xsl:for-each select="emblem:motto/emblem:transcription">
<xsl:if test="normalize-space(string(.)) != ''">
<div class="font-16" property="s:hasPart" typeof="s:CreativeWork">
<span class="emptySpan" property="s:additionalType" resource="http://
emblematica.library.illinois.edu/schemas/emb/EmblemTextPart"> </
span>
<span class="emptySpan" property="s:additionalType" resource="http://
emblematica.library.illinois.edu/schemas/emb/Motto"> </span>
```

```
<xsl:choose>
<xsl:when test="@xml:lang = 'de'">
<div class="col-sm-3">
<span class="indent" property="s:inLanguage" content="{@xml:lang}">
<xsl:text>German (Original): </xsl:text>
</span>
</div>
<div class="col-sm-9" property="s:text">
<xsl:value-of select="normalize-space(text()[1])"/>
</div>
<xsl:if test="emblem:normalisation">
<div class="col-sm-3" >
<span class="indent">
<xsl:text>German (Normalized): </xsl:text>
</span>
</div>
<div class="col-sm-9" property="e:normalizedText">
<xsl:value-of select="normalize-space(emblem:normalisation/text())"/>
</div>
</xsl:if>
</xsl:when>
<xsl:otherwise>
<xsl:if test="@xml:lang">
<div class="col-sm-3" property="s:inLanguage" content="{@xml:lang}">
<span class="indent">
<xsl:choose>
<xsl:when test="@xml:lang = 'la'">Latin</xsl:when>
<xsl:when test="@xml:lang = 'en'">English</xsl:when>
<xsl:when test="@xml:lang = 'nl'">Dutch</xsl:when>
<xsl:when test="@xml:lang = 'it'">Italian</xsl:when>
<xsl:when test="@xml:lang = 'fr'">French</xsl:when>
<xsl:when test="@xml:lang = 'el'">Greek</xsl:when>
<xsl:when test="@xml:lang = 'es'">Spanish</xsl:when>
</xsl:choose>
<xsl:text>: </xsl:text>
</span>
</div>
</xsl:if>
<div class="col-sm-9" property="s:text">
<xsl:value-of select="text()"/>
</div>
</xsl:otherwise>
</xsl:choose>
</div>
</xsl:if>
```

```
</xsl:for-each>
</div>
<div class="row">
<div class="col-sm-3">
<span class="font-20">Persistent Link:</span>
</div>
<div class="col-sm-9">
<a class="font-16">
<xsl:attribute name="href">
<xsl:value-of select="@globalID"/>
</xsl:attribute>
<xsl:value-of select="@globalID"/>
</a>
</div>
</div>
</div>
</xsl:template>
<xsl:template name="string-replace-all">
<xsl:param name="text" />
<xsl:param name="replace" xml:space="preserve" />
<xsl:param name="by" />
<xsl:choose>
<xsl:when test="$text = '' or $replace = '' or not($replace)" >
<xsl:value-of select="$text" />
</xsl:when>
<xsl:when test="contains($text, $replace)">
<xsl:value-of select="substring-before($text,$replace)" />
<xsl:value-of select="$by" />
<xsl:call-template name="string-replace-all">
<xsl:with-param name="text" select="substring-after($text,$replace)" />
<xsl:with-param name="replace" select="$replace" />
<xsl:with-param name="by" select="$by" />
</xsl:call-template>
</xsl:when>
<xsl:otherwise>
<xsl:value-of select="$text" />
</xsl:otherwise>
</xsl:choose>
</xsl:template>
</xsl:stylesheet>
```

APPENDIX

Software Configurations for Working with XML, XSD, XSLT, and XQuery

This appendix provides tips and instructions for downloading, installing, configuring, and using select XML, XSD, XSLT, and XQuery software. Implementers have several good software options, both free and commercial. See chapter 12 for information about additional tools and other useful XML resources.

SyncRO Soft oXygen

oXygen is a commercial, general-purpose XML editing and development tool. It is used to create and edit XML and HTML, as well as to create and test XML schemas, XPath expressions, XSLT stylesheets, and XQuery. It has aggressive academic pricing and a thirty-day free trial license.

- Product home page: www.oxygenxml.com.
- Download from: www.oxygenxml.com/download_oxygenxml_editor .html. Please read the minimum requirements before installing. Both Windows and Mac operating systems are supported. Both options require Java (included as part of the oXygen download in case you do not already have a current version of Java installed).
- Windows 32-bit and 64-bit downloads are self-extracting install executables (.exe files). After download, run (double-click) the file and follow the install wizard instructions.
- Mac download is a zip file or a tar-gzip file. Once downloaded, installation is accomplished by unzipping or extracting in the usual way.

- In order to use oXygen (all platforms), you must paste in a valid license key. Keys are e-mailed to you. The first time you start oXygen, you will be prompted to paste in the key you were e-mailed. Simply copy and paste.
- To register for a thirty-day trial license key, go to www.oxygenxml.com/register.html. You can also request a trial license key or update your key by selecting 'Register . . .' from the 'Help' menu.
- For academic pricing: www.oxygenxml.com/buy_new_licenses_academic.html.

MarcEdit

MarcEdit is a freeware utility software application that is used by many catalogers and metadata librarians who routinely work with MARC records. It was developed by Terry Reese. These instructions are known to work with version 6.3x (released on April 16, 2017).

- General download information is available from http://marcedit.reeset.net/downloads. The simple freeware license is here: http://marcedit.reeset.net/marcedit-end-user-license-agreement.
- Download for Windows 32-bit operating system: http://marcedit.reeset.net/software/MarcEdit_Setup.msi.
- Simply save the appropriate file to your computer, run it, agree to the license, and tell the installer where to put the application on your file system (hard drive).
- Download for Windows 64-bit operating system: http://marcedit.reeset.net/software/MarcEdit_Setup64.msi.
- Simply save this file to your computer, run it, agree to the license, and tell the installer where to put the application.
- Download for Mac OXS, version 10.6 and later:
    - The Mono Framework, version 3.4 or later, must be installed first.
    - Get and run the self-installing package (.pkg file) for Mac OSX from here: www.mono-project.com/download.
    - Then download MarcEdit: http://marcedit.reeset.net/software/MarcEdit_app.zip.

- Install by unzipping.
- Run MarcEdit by clicking on the MarcEdit app.

(Detailed instructions: http://marcedit.reeset.net/marcedit-mac-installation-instructions)

Web Browsers

Most modern web browsers, including Chrome, Explore, and Safari, will display raw XML (as shown in figure Appendix D.1), and many will also display styled XML as transformed by an XSLT stylesheet (e.g., into HTML, as shown in figure Appendix D.2).

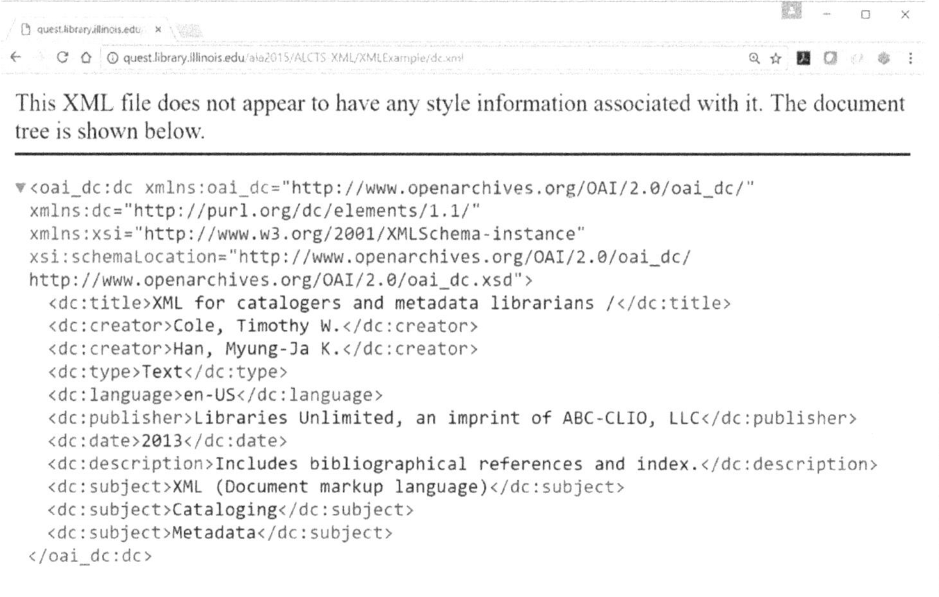

Figure Appendix D.1 | **Display of a raw XML file in Chrome (Windows 10)**

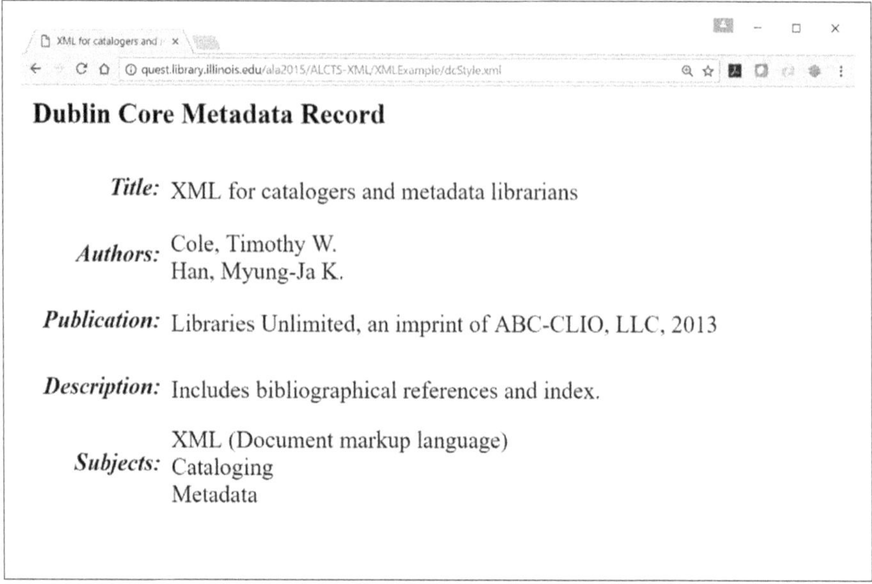

Figure Appendix D.2 | **Display of an XML file after styling by XSLT in Explore (Windows 10)**

Plain Text Editors

Any plain text editor can be used to create and edit XML files, but avoid word processors (like MS Word) which introduce special formatting characters into files when saved. Also, some plain text editors do a better job of displaying XML to make editing easier. A few good plain text editors to consider are listed below. These are free/shareware and are easy to install. However, these tools do not have the test and debugging features available in oXygen.

- Adobe Brackets for Mac and Windows (Adobe Systems, Inc.)
  - Website: http://brackets.io/
  - Optimized for editing HTML, CSS, JavaScript, and so on, but color coding works well for creating well-formed XML and XSLT as well.
- Notepad++ for Windows (Don Ho)
  - Website: http://notepad-plus-plus.org/
  - As above, but with a few more options regarding encoding, coding language, display, and so on.

- GNU Emacs, multiple operating systems (Free Software Foundation)
    - Website: https://www.gnu.org/software/emacs/
    - Works on many different platforms for a wide range of markup and coding languages, but Emacs began in the 1970s; many users today find the interface and advanced features of Emacs challenging to use and nonintuitive. For the novice, Emacs is only appropriate for simple, straightforward XML editing.

XML Spy

XML Spy XML Editor (Altova) is a good full-feature XML editing tool that some prefer to oXygen.

- Website: www.altova.com/xmlspy.html
- Full range of functionality, comparable to oXygen, with modest, mostly easy-to-recognize differences in look and feel.
- Educational discounts available (www.altova.com/edu-partnership.html)
- Thirty-day free trial available (www.altova.com/download-trial.html)
- Installation similar to oXygen, but follow the instructions on the website.

Stylus Studio

Stylus Studio XML Editor comes in three versions at various price points, including an inexpensive Home Edition. But the Home Edition version does not support XQuery and a number of other advanced features.

- Website: www.stylusstudio.com/ (also: www.stylusstudio.com/buy/ and www.stylusstudio.com/buy/compare.html)
- Professional and Enterprise versions comparable to oXygen and XML Spy; the Home Edition has fewer features, but most of what will be needed for the workshop
- Academic pricing available (www.stylusstudio.com/buy/academic_pricing.html)
- Fifteen-day free trial available (www.stylusstudio.com/xml_download.html)

BaseX (XQuery)

Programming is a hands-on activity and is best learned by doing. To get started with using XQuery, you need a programming environment, a place to write and run queries. The best open-source tool for beginners is BaseX. It is an easy-to-use XQuery processor.

Download and Install BaseX

- First, for both Windows/Mac environments, check to make sure Java 7 is installed on your computer, since Java 7 is required for the current version of BaseX.
- Go to http://basex.org/ to download the latest version (currently BaseX 8.6.3). Choose Download BaseX: http://basex.org/products/download/all-downloads/.

Windows Installation

- Choose the Windows Installer BaseX 8.6.3.exe to download and install BaseX.
- After downloading, double-click the BaseX863.exe file and follow the installation instructions.
- Double-click the BaseX icon to open the BaseX GUI (GUI is an acronym for "graphical user interface").

Mac Installation

- Choose the Core Package BaseX 8.6.3.jar to download BaseX.
- After downloading, double-click on the jar file in the Downloads folder.
- Go into Preferences/Security to confirm that you want to open this file for the BaseX GUI to open.
- While not required, to keep the BaseX installation, move the BaseX 8.6.3.jar file to the Applications folder.

Another Option for Mac Computers

- Choose Other Distributions => Mac OSX (Homebrew).
- For Mac users, it is recommended to install BaseX using Homebrew.
- First, install homebrew (http://brew.sh/) using the command line.
- Then install BaseX (http://brewformulas.org/Basex) using the command line.
- Users will then need to start the application from the command line: basexgui.

Setting Up a Database of Metadata Records in BaseX

- The next step is to use a set of metadata records, that is, XML documents, to set up a database.
- In BaseX: Choose Database => New.
- On the General tab: under "Input file or directory:" browse to the location of your XML documents where they are stored on the file system.
- Under "Name of database:" provide a name of your choosing for the new database, for example, "mods-records".
- Then choose the Parsing tab and uncheck "Chop whitespaces," since we want to retain the whitespace in your XML documents; for example, for <nonSort>The </nonSort> we want to retain the space after "The".
- Click OK to complete the process. The database is now ready for writing and running queries.

Working in an XQuery Main Module

- The BaseX Editor view is the main module where you will write and run queries.
- Write your first query and click on the green arrow above the workspace to run it.

- View the result of your query in the Result view. Remember that unless you are using the XQuery Update expressions, you are not changing the underlying data.
- Save this query by selecting Editor => Save As => File name. Name your file; it will be saved with file extension .xq as an XQuery file.
- If you would like to simplify the BaseX workspace, go to View and only check off: Editor, Result, Buttons, and Status Bar. Not every view is needed for basic XQuery programming.
- This completes the preparation for the hands-on work with XQuery. Have fun!

ABOUT THE AUTHORS

TIMOTHY W. COLE is mathematics librarian and coordinator for library applications in the iSchool's Center for Informatics Research in Science and Scholarship at the University of Illinois at Urbana-Champaign. He is the coauthor of *XML for Catalogers and Metadata Librarians* (2013) and *Using the Open Archives Initiative Protocol for Metadata Harvesting* (2007) and has published widely on metadata, linked open data, and the use of XML in libraries. Cole is a past cochair of the W3C Web Annotation Working Group. A member of the University of Illinois faculty since 1989, Cole has held prior posts in the Library Systems Office and Engineering Library. He is the winner of the 2017 LITA/OCLC Kilgour Award.

MYUNG-JA ("MJ") K. HAN is a metadata librarian and associate professor of library administration at the University of Illinois at Urbana-Champaign. Her main responsibilities consist of developing, evaluating, and enhancing cataloging and metadata workflows. Her research interests include the interoperability of metadata, issues on bibliographic control in the digital library environment, and the semantic web and linked data. She has published papers in *Library Trends, Library Resources and Technical Services*, and the *Journal of Library Metadata* on metadata quality and bibliographic control.

CHRISTINE SCHWARTZ is metadata librarian and XML database administrator at the Princeton Theological Seminary. She has researched and written about cataloging trends and issues on her blog, *Cataloging Futures*. She contributed an essay, "Changing Mind-set, Changing Skill Set: Transitioning from Cataloger to Metadata Librarian," to the book *Conversations with Catalogers in the 21st Century* (2010). Schwartz served on the Code4Lib Journal Editorial Committee in 2008–2009. She has worked with the XQuery programming language for over nine years, specifically working with library metadata programmatically.

INDEX

Lightning Source UK Ltd.
Milton Keynes UK
UKHW02f2144270318
320129UK00005B/246/P

9 781783 303694